THE STRAIGHT LEFT AND HOW TO CULTIVATE IT

The Deluxe Edition

JIM DRISCOLL
Featherweight Champion of the World

PROMETHEAN PRESS

The Straight Left and How to Cultivate It: Deluxe Edition

Promethean Press
1846 Rosemeade Pkwy #192
Carrollton, TX 75007
www.promethean-press.com

Copyright © 2008 by Promethean Press

All rights reserved, including the right of reproduction in whole or in part in any form.

The text in this edition has been revised by Gilbert Odd.

Manufactured in the United States of America

ISBN 978-0-9810202-0-4

TABLE OF CONTENTS

Foreword	1
Chapter One: Why the Straight Left?	3
Chapter Two: Its Erroneous Use	11
Chapter Three: Cultivation of Straight Hitting	27
Chapter Four: Training for Straight Hitting	39
Chapter Five: Straight Left in Defence	51
Chapter Six: Straight Left in Attack	61
Chapter Seven: Countering the Straight Left	73
Addendum: Peerless Jim: The Life and Fights of Jim Driscoll	81

FOREWORD

I consider it a great honor to write the foreword to Jim Driscoll's book, *The Straight Left and How to Cultivate It*. Throughout history, some books stand out among others as masterpieces in their various fields. For the art of boxing, *The Straight Left* is such a book.

Many boxers have used this book as a guide and inspiration in their training. In *The Straight Left*, Jim Driscoll describes the simple straight left punch as a formidable and versatile weapon that can be used for a direct attack, as defense, and as a counterattack.

Bringing an unmatched scientific mind to the art of pugilism, Driscoll drew from the established science of fencing to find the root of effective striking and footwork. In his own words, boxing is simply "sword fencing without a sword".

Driscoll's development of the boxing arts made him virtually unmatched in his day and inspired generations of fighters after him, from heavyweight champions like Georges Carpentier to even the late, great martial artist Bruce Lee, whose own martial art of Jeet Kune Do (literally, "The Way of the Intercepting Fist") borrowed heavily from Driscoll's boxing science, particularly the Straight Left punch.

A recurring theme in Driscoll's books, and one that will be found once more in the pages that follow, is his passionate defense of British boxers in a time where their dominance of the art was at a decline. In *The Straight Left*, Jim Driscoll explains why the Straight Left was abandoned by the boxers of his time and how that led to the domination of American boxers over the British. Driscoll argues that it is only the Straight Left that can allow British boxers to overcome American boxers, a theory he proved time and time again in the ring.

I hope you enjoy this book and learn the lessons shared from a great boxer like Jim Driscoll. His boxing as well as his literary achievements show why Jim Driscoll was truly a great champion in and out of the ring.

Richard Torres
New York

CHAPTER ONE
WHY THE STRAIGHT LEFT?

That a book of instruction in boxing should be devoted to the teaching of but one particular blow may need some explanation, although the average person who is in any way interested in the "Noble Art" must be fully aware of the value and importance of the good old straight left. It is the oldest blow in boxing; the first blow ever struck by the pioneers of fisticuffs when the sport evolved from crude fighting and became a scientific art.

It is the opening gambit in any contest with the gloves, for only the veriest novice or the rough-and-tumble scrapper ever attempts to lead with the right. The perfect mastery of the straight left is the first essential to success in boxing and despite the changes of style that have been seen since the game has become so commercialised, it still remains the orthodox point-scoring blow and the principal match-winning delivery that so often paves the way for the more spectacular punch from either left or right that brings a contest to a summary conclusion.

In the very beginnings of boxing the knockout, so ardently expected and anticipated by the modern spectator, was by no means the main attraction as it is today. Boxing was styled "The Noble Art of Self-Defence" and each contest was an exhibition between two students of the art to determine the more skillful of the pair. If during the course of the exchanges one of the participants was put down or so severely punished that he failed to continue that was merely incidental, and was not the principal objective of the contestants.

Naturally, there were other blows from the left hand that were brought into use and an equal number employing the right, but the basic delivery was the straight left lead which owed its supreme importance to the fact that in boxing, as distinctly opposed to fencing, the left foot is extended towards the opponent, the left side of the body turned towards him and thus the extended left arm automatically becomes the speediest and most natural way of reaching him.

But why the *straight* left? Why not the swing, which must surely gather power in its path or the hook, which can be whipped in with disturbing effect? Well, the answer is as old as Euclid, who told us that the shortest distance between two points is the straightest. However speedy the boxer may be in the delivery of his punches the undeniable fact remains that the straight blow is the quickest of all because it travels the shortest distance.

Nowadays it is found that the exponent of the straight left is not fully appreciated by the majority of fight spectators. They have been educated into a fanatical desire to see two-fisted, non-stop action that is far removed from the original scientific art. A modern boxing tournament is no longer an exhibition of skilled fisticuffs, which would no doubt be found more than a trifle slow in these days of hustle and bustle, but in spite of this change the straight left is indisputably the best weapon, both in defence and attack, as the master boxer and the intelligent onlooker realise to their benefit and satisfaction.

The purpose of this textbook therefore is to justify the straight left and to enable aspiring boxers, both amateur and professional, to bring its use to the acme of perfection. If it is made the premier stroke in the repertoire of a glove exponent his work will bear the hallmark of a champion even if he never manages to reach that pinnacle of fame. Moreover, by bringing its exploitation to perfection he will assuredly beat many more opponents than beat him, and when his ring career has been concluded will hang up his gloves with his mental and physical capacities entirely unimpaired.

As another argument in favour of the straight left, may I cite my own case. I started boxing before I was fifteen for the sheer love of it. I became a club fighter in my native town and when I had progressed sufficiently as an amateur I went into a booth which toured Wales and the neighbouring towns, where I engaged in a vast number of unrecorded contests against all comers, irrespective of size and weight. From 1901 until 1919 I fought both in Great Britain and America against the leading men in the world at my weight, and of sixty-one recorded contests I lost only three. One of these was on a debatable decision, which was afterwards reversed; the second was by disqualification and the third (my last appearance in the ring) when I attempted to "come back" after a lengthy absence, and was a sick man. During the years 1914-1918 I was boxing instructor in the army and had the gloves on almost daily with a never-ending stream of ambitious do-or-die scrappers.

Yet, after nearly a quarter-of-a-century of activity within the roped arena I left the game without a mark on my face or body to advertise the nature of my arduous profession, in fact, in ordinary clothing I looked less like a retired champion boxer than anything else. For this and to the successes I achieved with the gloves I am indebted to the straight left, the value of which from the very start I was fortunate enough to discover and straightaway set about to develop to the highest possible degree.

I have many times been asked why it is that a boxer takes up the left foot forward stance and why he extends his left arm in preference to his right and uses the left as his principal scoring weapon. The natural fighter always strikes with his right and stands with his right foot foremost, yet any boxer who takes up this stance is thought to look awkward and is considered to be unorthodox. In boxing parlance he is called a "south-paw". My answer to this somewhat puzzling query is that the originator of boxing as a sport - the art of self-defence - was James Figg, always regarded as the first champion of England. He introduced bare-knuckle fighting at his school of arms in the Tottenham Court Road, London, and it became very popular among the sporting gentry of the day. Figg's academy was ostensibly for the teaching of sword and cudgel play and quarter staff, and this no doubt explains why he applied the principles of fencing to the new art of boxing.

While it had taken several decades to determine the best stance for fencing, the position for boxing was discovered more readily. At the outset no doubt, Figg caused his pupils to take up the fencing position, right leg advanced, right arm held ready for striking and he probably taught them to hit in a perfectly straight line as if making a sword thrust. To guard themselves they used the same arm to parry the blows from an opponent, while the left formed an additional shield. The fencing professors plumped for the right foot forward stance because the heart being on the left side (as they thought in those days), was then kept furthest from the point of the sword. As the science developed it was decided that the heart could be better protected from a right-hand punch if the left arm was extended, this being in addition a guard for a blow aimed at the head. They also found that the boxer could hit equally as hard, if not harder, with his right from the left foot stance, while the same arm provided an effective shield if held up while the left was being used to stab off an opponent who was about to launch his right. And very soon they came to the conclusion that a straight left blow always reached its target before one from the right could be landed by a rival. The science of boxing continued to develop and was passed on from Figg to such noteworthy exponents of fisticuffs as Jim Ward, Mendoza, Jack Broughton (who drew up the original prize ring rules), Jim Belcher, and so on down to Jem Mace, the last and probably the cleverest of those great bare-knuckle fighters. Boxing was originally the prerogative of the British, who made a sport of it and taught it to the rest of the world. At one time every British champion was automatically a world's champion, but not even a proportionate share of these coveted titles come our way today. It is with the idea of restoring British boxing to its rightful place that this book has been written, for I am confident that only by acquiring mastery in the use of the straight left can our boxers ever hope to hold their own and triumph over the best glove exponents in the world.

Jack Broughton (1734-1750), father of first boxing rules.

CHAPTER TWO
ITS ERRONEOUS USE

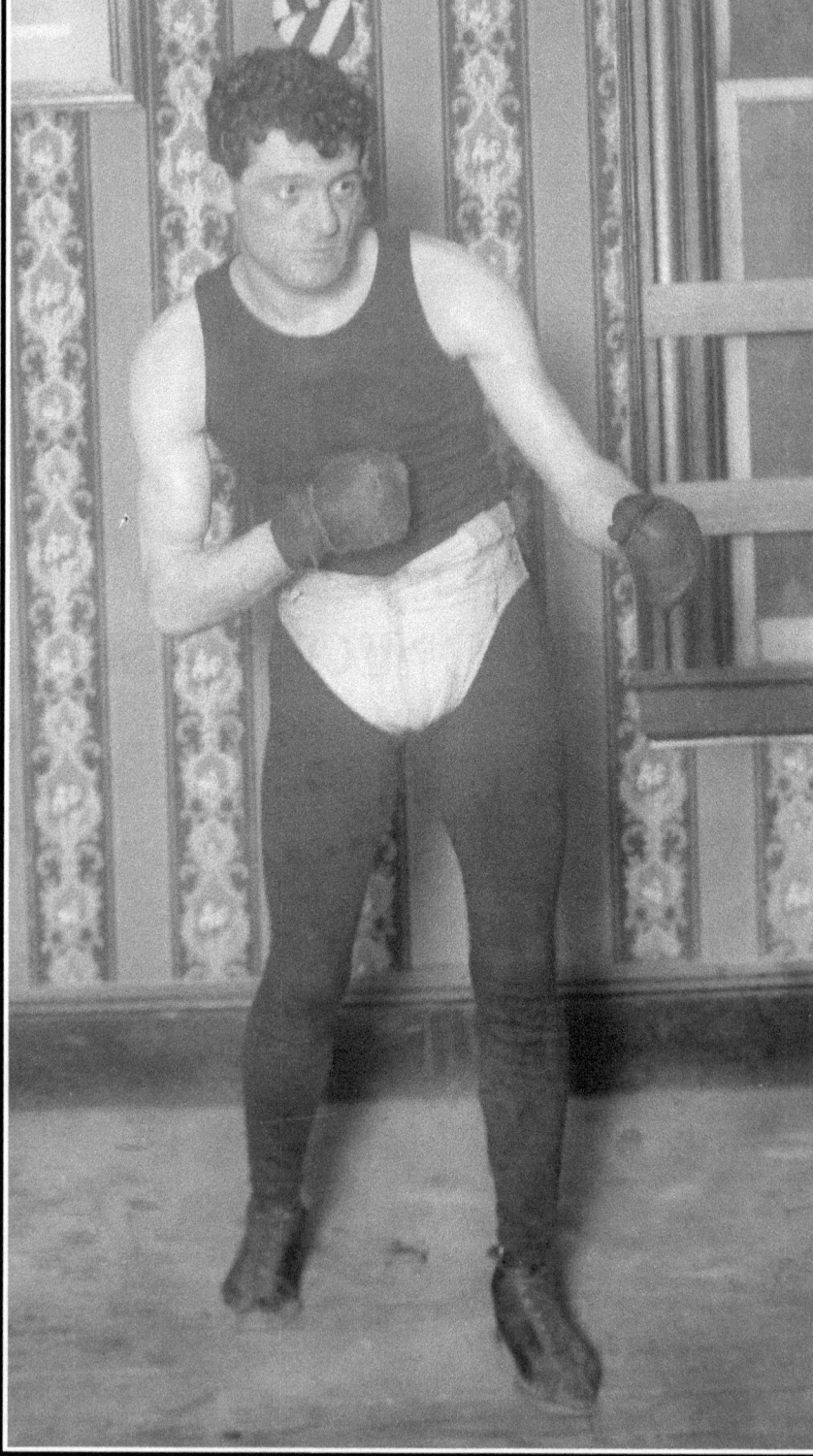

As pointed out in the previous chapter, the British style was the orthodox method practised by all performers in the ring, simply and solely because the sport was confined to this country. The straight left was unquestionably the principal weapon for both attack and defence and was accepted as such by each and every country which eventually adopted the game. Then came the time when these countries began sending their leading boxers to these shores to give combat to our champions and we suffered shock after shock as our best men in the various weight divisions were sent down to defeat. Worse than that, when we really thought we had discovered some outstanding talent and sent it abroad to retrieve our lost laurels, in most cases the expedition was fruitless and gradually the high prestige that once surrounded a boxer bearing the title of British champion slumped to a pitifully low level.

Naturally, this was most noticeable in the case of America, where boxing reached the summit of popularity. Fighters from the United States defeated our best men far too frequently, while of those British boxers who ventured to seek fame and fortune in American rings only a bare handful achieved their ambitions and won world's titles.

This state of affairs led to the conclusion that the one time pre-eminence of the upstanding straight-hitting British style was a thing of the past. The American method, although modelled on the original, was proving far superior and our fighting men were strongly urged to drop the straight left and all that it implied, and go in for two-fisted, non-stop tactics and let out-fighting be forsaken in favour of in-fighting.

This was, of course, quite an erroneous idea and the worst sort of advice to give. The British style was by no means out-of-date and had not been superseded by the methods employed by successful American boxers. The fact was that our own performers had in the main allowed themselves to drift into slipshod methods that had become but a parody of the original British style, while far from inventing a new style, the Americans were putting over a more thorough rendering of the methods they had learned from us.

How had this come about? Jem Mace, termed by many as the "Father of British Boxing", was a faithful exponent of the upstanding British style and apart from holding the heavyweight championship of this country had a very substantial claim to the world's title. When Mace retired undefeated he journeyed to Australia and there passed on his fistic knowledge to a certain Larry Foley, who later on opened his famous school of boxing in Sydney. Mace also ran a boxing saloon and the great Bob Fitzsimmons first came into notice there by winning a competition.

Jem Mace

But Foley made fame as a teacher and such world-beaters as Peter Jackson, Dan Creedon, Jim Hall, and Young Griffo, in addition to Fitzsimmons, learnt the art of self-defence from him, and proceeding to the United States, passed on their methods to those American battlers who were quick enough to realise its potentialities and adapt them to their existing methods. Thus came the time when British boxers were being regularly beaten at their own game by others who were putting over a superior interpretation of it.

There were, of course, American fighters who won over our men, both at home and in this country, on sheer aggressiveness. These were fierce-hitting tough guys whose dynamic and concentrated attacking proved too much for anyone not their equal in strength and durability, even if they were surpassed in the scientific side of the business, or that degree of boxing skill possessed by their victims, but which, because of imperfections was not sufficient to stave off defeat. But in the majority of instances the Americans who came, saw and conquered, together with those who so successfully performed at home against British competition, were men of outstanding boxing skill, into which they had infused a high degree of forcibleness and the maximum of punching power. Furthermore, they knew the value of straight-left hitting and were experts in the manner in which they employed this all-important blow.

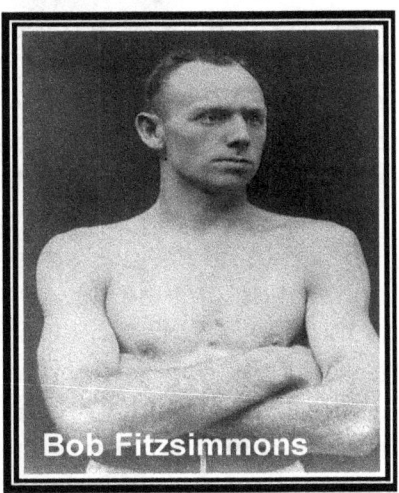
Bob Fitzsimmons

They were dubbed "box-fighters", because they combined the qualities of both styles of performer and their records show that not only were they infinitely superior to the inept straight-lefter, but were always able to cope with the roughest and toughest of their fellow-countrymen. All of which goes to show that the exponent of the straight left who really knows how to use that weapon, who has the sense to combine with it a first-rate knowledge of the original upstanding British style and who hits hard and often, can set a course that leads direct to a world's championship.

Another reason for the assumption that the straight left had seen its day was the success of those Americans who made in-fighting their principal means of securing victory. First and foremost they were tough in every description of the word. They trained assiduously and built up a muscular development to withstand the hardest hammering they could expect to receive; they attained a high degree of staying power; provided themselves with a heavy punch in either hand; made attack their sole method of defence and went into action with the one idea of battering down the opposition in the quickest possible time.

They brought in-fighting to a fine art. As soon as the gong sounded to start a contest they sought close quarters immediately and relied for their success on their ability to assimilate punishment and to deal it out. They scorned the use of the straight left or professed to do so. Some of them actually did, relying on swings, hooks and particularly on rough tactics to smash their way to victory. And they were generally successful over the "straight-lefters", who came up against them, not because their "American" style was superior, but because they were stronger and tougher men physically, and because the British stylists whom they met and defeated were only half-educated pugilistically. These so-called exponents of the British style might have been able to hit straight, but were ignorant or indifferent to the necessity of putting real force into their punches as well as accuracy of aim.

Sad to relate, this state of affairs exists today, and will go on existing until our boxers realise that while the straight left is the best medium of all for scoring points and winning contests, it can only remain so when scientifically delivered with the full bodyweight behind the blow and sent home on those targets that are most vulnerable. Instead, we find that the youths who endeavour to make good in this country are usually content to fall into clinches at each and every opportunity, to hold and to wrestle, to slap and to dab freely to the discredit of the game itself and to the wreck of their own opportunities for self-advancement.

The youthful boxer who sets out to really cultivate the use of the straight left and learns how to punch hard and accurately with it need never fear the outcome of a contest with the rough-and-tumble fighter who relies more on brute force than anything else to win his battles. This type of ringster follows a plan of campaign which has as its ultimate object the laying low of his opponent. How this is to be brought about hardly matters and he will use every variety of punch, effective or otherwise, hit from all angles and generally trust to luck until his purpose is achieved, taking care meanwhile to see that any minor infringement of the rules that may creep into his tactics escapes the notice of the referee.

But this represents the sum total of his repertoire. He throws punches in windmill fashion and he puts weight behind them, but the man who picks his punch up from whatever position his hand may be in and who brings it over in the pious hope that it may prove to be a winner, is taking a big gamble. This type of battler is apt to declare that he picks his pet punches off the floor, meaning that he packs into their delivery every ounce of weight that can be secured. But how often does he connect with those heavy thumps? Any boxer with a fair knowledge of the game and who is smart with his feet and has any idea of evasiveness should not be caught by such haphazard blows, which can only be really effective against a stationary target.

One thing more. All punches should be picked off the floor, as I will show later on. But not the way of doing so that the rough-and-tumble fighter uses. He disregards all that is scientific about the delivery of a blow and is consequently an easy problem for the stylist who has mastered the art of straight hitting, accuracy of aim and perfect timing. To put the argument another way, the determined two-fisted battlers, so cherished by the misguided spectators of today, can be rated as bludgeon fighters, who disdain the use of the rapier, for the simple reason that they are utterly ignorant of the finer points of the game. Yet the whole history of single combat refutes their chosen style. Man did not abandon the club as a weapon because he preferred the rapier as a parlour pastime, but because the sword proved itself to be the more useful weapon. And it was by a similar process of discovery that the axe, which had superseded the club, gave way to the sword and buckler, then to the case of swords, until even the broadsword and sabre were abandoned in favour of the rapier.

This evolution of the sword is well worthy of study, since it forms an exact parallel in the history of the fist as the weapon of single combat. For though the ingenious novelists have perhaps frequently strained the truth when relating how

their academically trained heroes have prostrated some half-a-dozen uncouth bullies with the greatest ease owing to their knowledge of the fistic art, there has nevertheless been a foundation of both truth and plausibility for these adventures.

Fistic science, if backed by strength and intelligence, ought always to beat brute force, and will even triumph in a rough-and-tumble, although when the rough-and-tumble arrives the scientific boxer will find that it is necessary to employ similar tactics himself as well as more orthodox methods. Science wins because the rapier can be made to get home more frequently and more accurately than the club. But it must be got home to good purpose, and must be both intelligently and forcefully directed.

Let every aspiring boxer realise that he will be beaten, not only by the tough, heavy-hitting swinger and in-fighter, but by the exponent of orthodox out-fighting, unless he himself masters the art of hitting hard as well as accurately and builds up physical and nervous strength to enable him to take whatever happens to come his way. But more than that let him realise that boxing is "the noble art of self-defence", that it has always borne that name and that its practice and study is still recommended on this sole plea. He should also remember, however, that defence is not only the chief thing to be considered, but that attack can only be allowed to come into the picture at all when it is employed as an auxiliary to defence and that the strongest form of defence is a vigorous attack, carried out mainly and almost entirely with a view to the minimising of the risk, or the repulse, of all counter-attack. And this is where the straight left comes in. Not, as is usually supposed, mainly as a mode of attack, but rather as a more effective and valuable means of keeping an opponent at a respectable distance. As already observed, the science of modern boxing, as instituted by Figg and Broughton, was and always has been a material development of the art of fencing. It is practically sword fencing without a sword and in all its movements follows, or rather should follow, the same principles.

Now, as most people are aware, the very first principle of fencing is that the student must learn to "keep the line". For as long as he can contrive to preserve a straight wall of steel in a direct line from his shoulder down to his arm, so long will his body be impregnable to attack. The whole aim of attack in sword play is to get past this line, for until it is passed no point can be made. In earlier sword play, where a buckler, second sword, dagger or cloak was held in or wrapped round the left hand, there used to be a second line of defence, but it was always intended that the sword should be the principal barrier of protection and it is, I believe, generally admitted that the science of the sword never approached perfection until the sword became the sole weapon of both attack and defence.

Boxing does differ in this respect, inasmuch as the elimination of the right hand for either attack or defence is practically unthinkable. But for all that, the right hand should be invariably regarded as quite a secondary affair. It is a reinforcing weapon pure and simple, one that should be used in much the same way as the dagger was used in the old days of sword and dagger combat, save and except that the right hand is, and must necessarily be, more frequently employed to give the *coup de grace* than the dagger ever used to be.

There have been and always will be so-called boxers who will win contests almost solely by the use of the right hand, but these victories can only be won over opponents whose left-hand work is of such distinctly inferior order, or the force of which has been sapped by a series of fierce aggressions which have worn down their owners' stamina. Lucky, or so-called lucky, right-hand punches need not be considered, for unless these get home on a man who has had the misfortune to slip, there are really no such things as lucky punches.

It is true that a boxer may quite frequently send home a winning blow, the result of which will surprise him as well as it surprises the recipient, but any and every success of this description can only occur through some defect or failure of the loser's defence. The so-called lucky punch, however wild or unorthodox it may be, should, and can always be guarded against. Even the right cross, which has been justly and generally held to be the most effective punch in the whole catalogue, can only be effectively brought into operation after preliminary skillful play with the left. The left hand must prepare a way for it, either by a series of feints or stabs - though footwork, swerving, clinching and slipping (all branches of footwork by the way), will exert their influences. All others are, however, subsidiary to the work of the left hand. For the right-hand winning punches, "the auctioneers", as Tom Sayers styled them, can never be sent home until the receiver has been drawn inside the sphere of their operation, or, in other words until the line of his defensive, established and maintained by his left arm, has been carried.

In this respect more than in any other, the comparison between the case of the left hand and that of the sword in sword play holds good. The fencer is taught to keep the line, and has to learn that nothing else matters so much as this. In fact, that nothing else really matters at all. For if the line be always preserved, he cannot be touched. And as with the fencer, so with the boxer. So long as the latter maintains his line, *i.e.*, keeps that straight left of his shooting in and out, and his opponent at the business end of it, the other fellow will be powerless or practically powerless to do him any harm. One must either circumvent a straight left, or else force one's way through its defence, and the first of these feats can only be accomplished by compelling it to deviate from the straight line, or, in other words, to cease to he a straight left, while, if one wants to break through, one can only do so by running a most serious risk of being knocked out oneself, or in any case, undergoing a very severe and almost certain punishment for one's recklessness - always providing of course, that the straight-lefter lands a real punch with this weapon. For that is as important an essential of left-hand play as its accuracy. No matter how straight it may be, nor how frequently it may shoot out, the left hand punch is of precious little use as an offensive weapon, and even absolutely useless as a defensive one unless it is capable of checking an attack and even of stopping most attacks. My advice to boxers can be summed up thus: Hit first, hit hard and hit often, not forgetting also, to hit straight.

From the foregoing it will be appreciated that the boxer who makes an intense study of straight-left hitting and brings his performance as near to perfection as possible stands in little danger of being defeated, leave alone knocked out, until the time comes when he is opposed by one whose use of the straight left is superior to his own. Yet, time and time again, it is found that an exponent of the upstanding British style, who appears to be making every use of a straight left, gets beaten by a rival apparently far inferior in boxing skill and whose chief asset is the non-stop delivery of weighty punches. Why is it?

In the first place, it is of little use employing a straight left unless the following essential features are observed. It must be *straight*; it must be delivered with the full bodyweight behind it; it must be accurately aimed; it must be sent in with speed and it must connect with the knuckle portion of the fist. Far too many self-termed straight-lefters get the mistaken idea into their heads that they have merely to flick out their left arms to within an inch of an opponent's nose and the referee will immediately credit them with having scored. Some of them do not even bother to close their gloves, but use the extended fingers as a means of reaching the objective rather than step in and bang home a solid blow. Others, sad to relate, have even been seen to flagrantly flap or dab in the direction of a rival and then appear astounded when, in spite of these ridiculous efforts the other man has, after many rounds of this sort of opposition, been able to step in and put over a weighty punch that has brought a summary halt to the proceedings.

A genuine straight left should not only pull up an attacking opponent in his stride but at the same time jar him to his heels. It should be so well-timed as to reach its mark at the utmost of its owner's power, that is, with the maximum reach at his command, including shoulder extension, a movement that comes up his right leg, across his shoulders and along his left arm. It should strike home with the back knuckles of the closed fist and not cease on impact, but be followed through, just as a cricketer making a drive or a golfer executing a swing follows through the stroke to ensure full force and accuracy. Such a straight left will arrive home with shocking result upon an adversary and if blows of this nature are banged in as often as opportunity occurs it will not be long before the recipient's powers of resistance are reduced to the barest minimum and he becomes an easy target for either a well-timed right cross, a left hook or a similar destructive blow that will bring the contest to a decisive end.

It is the utterly futile use of the straight left by the majority of our boxers that has brought about the decline of British boxing and the condemnation of the once preeminent British style, and until every youth with ambitions towards winning fame and fortune in the ring realises this fact and resolves to make the straight left the foremost weapon in his fistic armoury, we shall continue to take a second, third, or even

fourth place among the boxing countries, which positions we have held at varying times since the roar of the crowd apparently persuaded our boxers to forego their heritage and adopt a style that they deem more colourful.

How mistaken is such an idea. What is more colourful, if one must use such a word, than the sight of an upstanding boxer, using brilliant footwork and body evasion, literally boxing rings round a forceful, lunging and wild hitting rival? It is a joy to watch such a performance and those who really understand the science of self-defence appreciate it to the full. Of course, a lot of trouble is due to the fact that in these days of big attendances (very profitable days for the modern fighter), the majority of the spectators do not know sufficient concerning the fundamentals of the art. But again, this is entirely the fault of the performers, who, in their incorrect performances of their native style, have given the impression that it is out of fashion and consequently redundant.

In following chapters I will endeavour to show how the straight left can be cultivated, how it should be used, and when. But in this chapter on its erroneous use I cannot come to a conclusion without warning the reader that unless he assiduously studies the other effective blows that come within the scope of a champion boxer's repertoire, all his work towards the effectiveness of the straight left will be wasted. Furthermore, I need hardly stress the importance of physical development as another vital accessory. There must be sufficient muscularity, of the right sort, to enable blows to be struck with the maximum of power and speed; there must be a strong nervous system to withstand shock and a strong constitution as well. Moreover, he must possess a degree of stamina that will carry him through an hour's arduous fighting if necessary, for every championship contest demands fifteen rounds of three minutes each duration, all of which calls for scientific and conscientious training.

In other words, there is nothing easy about boxing, but the rewards to those who are determined to make good are well worth the sweat and toil which the novice must undergo if he is to achieve his highest ambitions. As an amateur he will find plenty of fun, many friends and limitless self-satisfaction; as a professional he can make sufficient money in a short number of years which, if he is wise, will be there when he comes to hang up his gloves and enable him to follow the vocation of his choice. And what is of major importance, if he strictly adheres to the straight left as the basis of his work in the ring and endeavours to become a skilled boxer rather than a rugged fighter, he will find himself mentally and physically equipped to take up employment in another sphere when he eventually decides to quit the game as an active performer.

CHAPTER THREE
CULTIVATION OF STRAIGHT HITTING

While the young boxer may be ready and willing to accept the fact that the straight left is the speediest of all punches, simply because it has the shortest distance to travel, it is often difficult for him to appreciate the relative power of straight and round arm hitting. To him it seems so certain that a swing must necessarily be so much more forceful than a straight delivery and there is a lot of reason for this mistaken belief. The sensation of vigour suggested by a full revolution of the arm and the further sensation that every ounce of the weight of the body is being carried behind it as though it were being all thrown at the recipient, is so fascinating that he cannot resist the notion that a swinging punch must automatically be the more powerful.

As there are no similar sensations accompanying a straight lead or jab, or even a hook (which is, after all, but a variant of the straight punch), the novice is apt to pin his faith on swinging. Then, forgetting all about the need for accuracy, both in timing and aim, the risk of injury to the hands, or even the value of economy of time and balance, will continue to swing with more or less success at the expense of other swingers or of feeble straight punchers, until he has the misfortune to run up against a really accurate and forceful straight hitter and then meets with painful disaster without being able in the least to understand why or how.

For, quite apart from the loss of valuable time wasted by the swinging delivery, it is also practically impossible to aim a swing accurately. The swinger can only let one go in the hope that it will land there or thereabouts while, thanks partly to the time a swing occupies in starting and in delivery, the boxer who is temporarily filling the role of a target, is given many more opportunities of avoiding its arrival. The path of a swing can be gauged almost with certitude and consequently the man at whom it is aimed has the option of either jumping back out of its reach, of stepping in within its reach (so that the glove will pass round behind the back of his head), or of ducking under it. Either of these alternative courses will tend to disturb the swinger's balance and will therefore render him more or less at the other fellow's mercy, at least for a time. This is a disadvantage attending the swing which can never be attached to any straight punch, since, whether the latter be avoided by stepping back, by ducking or by a parry, the straight hitter can or should be able to recover his ground or position for attack or defence without the loss or waste of any appreciable time.

So it must be agreed that the use of the straight left saves time - a most valuable item in boxing as everyone will recognise; it also eliminates, to a large extent, the danger of losing balance, which is another all-important point to be remembered, for the maintenance of balance during the whole duration of a round is vitally necessary. In my view, true balance is the secret of success as a boxer, for without it the straight left, or any other punch for that matter, cannot be properly delivered, cannot be accurately aimed, and cannot carry the maximum power at the command of its user. And now we come to the question of damaged hands, so prevalent among modern ringsters.

That the boxer of today suffers far more from damaged hands than his predecessors cannot be denied, but few observers or critics of the game would seem to have discovered the reason for this phenomenon. It has been suggested, much to my amusement I must confess, that it is due to the fact that the modern fighter puts extra force into his punching, but this is absurd on the face of it and is unsupported by the slightest evidence. The old-time prize-fighters and the early glove exponents always made a practice of hitting straight, landing their punches fairly and squarely with the knuckles of the hand, thereby taking the jar of the impact on the part best fitted by nature to support it. A swinging punch may land anyhow, and by no means infrequently with an open glove (which will, of course, minimise the effect of the blow, though it may increase (unfairly) the length of the reach).

It may arrive in such wise that only the thumb comes into

contact with the target at which it is aimed, with the result that, apart from losing in effectiveness, there is a great risk that the thumb is wrenched or even dislocated. In no possible instance can it arrive so as to enable the jar of the impact being properly distributed, as it should be, throughout the whole length of the arm. All the bones, sinews and muscles of the hand and arm have been so arranged and placed by nature as to withstand the effects of a hard punch when this is delivered straight and accurately, whereas when a swing is made the full jar of the impact has to be borne by the hand and wrist alone. The swinger's thumbs, hands or wrists must go in time and in short time at that and when it is considered that a boxer's hands are his principal stock-in-trade, this further overwhelming argument in favour of the straight delivery as opposed to the swing cannot be ignored.

Let me now proceed with instruction for the cultivation of left-hand hitting. In the first place it is essential that the hand is correctly closed in order to make a fist that on impact with its objective will strike home solidly with the back knuckles. Next comes the position of the hands when hitting to make certain that when aiming at the head or the body the back knuckles are the first portion of the fist to strike the target and reach it with the full bodyweight behind the blow. For a delivery to the head the list should be half-turned so that the back of the hand and the elbow are in line and the thumb uppermost. You will find many boxers, including those at the top of the tree, who favour turning the wrist so that the palm of the hand is underneath, but this makes the best position for straight-left hitting to the body where the blow is directed downwards. Other fighters prefer the position whereby the palm appears uppermost and while I am inclined to agree that this comes as a very unpleasant visitation, especially when driven under the nose, I hold the view that there is a risk of the front knuckles reaching the objective first and so acting as a buffer for the back knuckles which are not allowed to land with their full power.

At this point, I would clear up a point that seems to worry the novice boxer no little. He gets told by one instructor to keep his fist tightly clenched throughout the duration of each round, another will tell him to rest his hand as much as possible and only clench his fist when striking. Both are misleading in their advice. It is wrong for him to keep the hand tightly closed while in the ring as this only leads to fatigue of the hand, wrist and forearm, but it is equally incorrect to keep his hands relaxed and only close them when about to strike for there is a grave risk that in the hasty exchange of punches he might not fully close his glove, with the result that he either hits with the open glove or incurs a minor, but nevertheless embarrassing, injury. My advice is to keep the left hand tightly clenched all the time, except when parrying or intercepting a blow, it being readily appreciated that in the last instance the open glove provides more cover against a blow than a closed one.

And while on the subject of the opening and closing of the hand, let me digress for a moment from the straight left and put in a word of warning regarding the closing of the mouth when boxing. All the while you are in action keep the teeth tightly clenched, do not on any account let the lower jaw drop and the mouth hang open. A dislocated or fractured jaw can easily result from taking a punch with the chin loose and if you want proof of this just open your mouth and wag your head from side to side, then repeat the action with the jaw held tight. Again, the clenched jaw offers far tougher resistance to a blow than the loosely hung chin and many boxers have suffered the indignity of a knockout from a blow, the effects of which they could easily have shaken off had the punch landed on a solidly held lower jaw instead of one hanging loose.

Now we come to the correct delivery of the straight left. We have already decided that it is a more forceful delivery than the swing, having agreed that the blow which is sent home with all the support of the arm behind it must automat-

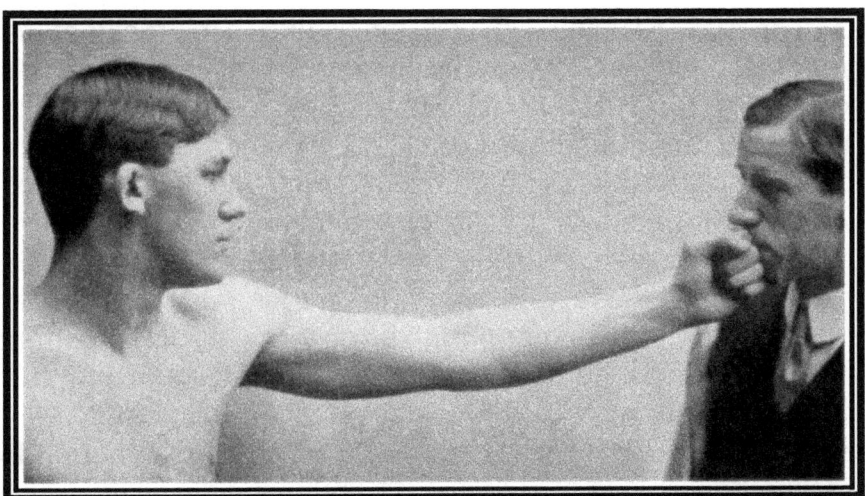

ically be more effective than one which has the support of the hand and wrist only. In fact, the power of the swing is vastly more apparent than real, whereas that of the straight punch is exactly the reverse - more real than apparent. It is, indeed, more certain of reaching its target, more easy to recover position from if its aim and force have been miscalculated, and it is finally both less injurious to the hands and more effective in its results.

But in order that it may possess all these advantages it must necessarily be accurate in its delivery, and it should, above all, be a real punch and not merely a push. The latter brand of delivery may score a few points, provided it actually reaches its objective, but it can never by any chance succeed in winning a contest if one's opponent is at all resolute. For no matter how unpolished or unscientific he may be, he can always afford to disregard a pushing or tapping left, and, without wasting time or energy in defence, can force his way in to certain victory. If, however, the straight left is to be regarded as the winning weapon it must of necessity be, first of all, *straight*, that is to say, accurately aimed, and this quality, simple and natural though it would appear, seems to be one which the average modern boxer finds most difficult to perform.

The main trouble, in my opinion, is due to the fact that the youngster who aspires to fistic fame usually picks up his knowledge from those of his club-mates likewise inclined and rarely has the benefit of a really qualified instructor. Few of our novices ever take the trouble to study a textbook on boxing with the result that their interpretation of correct stance and the delivery of a straight punch is merely what they have gleaned from those with whom they spar, who may be far from perfect in their performance of these vitally important matters. Those who by chance come under the watchful eye of an instructor who has in his day been a top-notch amateur or professional - and there are all too few of these about - do get the opportunity of starting right, but even these would be well advised to turn to the textbook in order to ensure the elimination of all error, for it is a definite fact that bad habits in boxing - as in every other walk of life - are particularly easy to pick up and extremely hard to lose.

Start by adopting the correct pose with which to open a contest. For the starting position in boxing you must be standing perfectly upright, with the weight on the left foot and your left hand held ready for the delivery of a sharp-shooting left to the chin. Take up this position, not only at the outset of a contest, but every time you are about to send out a left hand. In other words, do not adopt this classical pose at the commencement of the first round, then cheerfully forget all about it during the remainder of the contest. The right hand is not held in a threatening attitude, but kept ready to block your opponent's left or parry it (push it aside).

Now shoot out the left arm to its fullest extent, aiming at the nose of an imaginary rival. Make sure to get full shoulder extension, so that maximum reach is attained without going too far forward and so losing balance. Draw the arm back as a guard against any countering blow from your opponent's right and send it out again. Try this in a succession of shots when advancing and retreating, making certain that each movement is made with precision.

As a variation, practise shooting out a quick succession of blows, withdrawing the striking arm just sufficient so as to enable full power to be put behind each blow. Do not dab, but hit fiercely and determinedly with each delivery, always aiming in the centre of the face.

Let us next take the straight left to the body. Put in everything you've got when driving home a straight left to the mark and at the same time duck under your rival's attempted left lead to the head. To do this step in slightly to the right and sway over in the same direction to avoid his delivery. But whenever striking with the left, either to head or body, it is important to sway slightly to the right, if only by as much as dropping the right shoulder, as this adds to the driving power of the left. Try it for yourself and you will quickly realise this to the full.

Stand as nearly as possible edgewise to your opponent, have your weight evenly distributed on each leg, only shifting your balance to the left leg when striking or to the right leg when avoiding a punch without retreating. Keep erect on the balls of the feet, slightly jigging as if you were on springs; hold the left arm advanced, both as an offensive or defensive measure and loosely enough to enable you to check your opponent's attempts at aggression with a crisply delivered punch. In this position your left can alternately be used either by feints or actual offensive movements as a means of opening a breach for an attack on your own part.

Go after your man. Send out that left straight and true *and hard*; glide the left leg forward, bring up the right and in com-

plete coordination, bang in the left again. Follow up with a series of quick, yet methodically aimed, lefts, driving hard for the head until he raises his guard, then sinking one into his mid-section. As you move across the ring the sound of your feet should have a rhythmic beat and your left should shoot out like a piston-rod. Make every punch a decisive action, allow no blow to be sent out haphazardly. You won't score with every punch, but the accuracy and power behind each delivery will let your opponent see that you mean business and his sole thoughts will be concentrated on defence.

Do not be too eager to take part in an actual contest. You do not get a lot of time to study the art of self-defence when another fellow is in there fully determined to punch you on the nose as often as he is able. Of course, there is a great deal to learn from actual combat, but that is in the finishing stages of your fistic education. If you are too impatient to study or practise the arts of straight hitting and feinting for openings you will find yourself compelled to experience the difficulties of forcing a passage *through* the defence of your opponents and so tempted to try to discover a path *round* them. Then all that you have been told about straight hitting will be wasted and your prospects of reaching the top will be seriously impeded.

CHAPTER FOUR
TRAINING FOR STRAIGHT HITTING

We have already decided that there are four principles that govern straight hitting, *i.e.*, perfect balance of the body, accuracy of aim, precise timing and coordination, and maximum power of punch. Now we have to study the training methods for obtaining these qualities and we will take them in turn in the order I have listed them. The finest exercise for the development of a sense of balance is undoubtedly skipping. Not ordinary haphazard skipping, but the real thing. First, skip on one foot, holding the other in front of you; then skip on the other. After that skip on alternate feet with each revolution of the rope - not so simple as it may appear - and work up to the highest possible speed. Keep the skipping going for three minutes the duration of a round - then rest for a minute and skip for another three minutes. Three rounds of skipping in a variety of ways will form the opening for a good workout.

Here are some rhythmic exercises to aid balance and they should be carried out smoothly and follow one another without a break - about twelve times each exercise is sufficient. Start off with touching the toes - or as near to them as you can reach without bending the knees. Then, with the feet astride, touch the left toe with the left hand; at the same time swinging the right arm vertically overhead, then touch the right toe with the right arm, swinging the left arm as straight up as possible. Next, lie prone, heels together, and suddenly bring up the right leg as high as possible at the same time raising the trunk and swinging over the left hand to touch the right knee; repeat with the left leg being raised and touched by the right hand.

Stand in an upright position, arms at the sides and heels together. Now drop into a squat position, raising your heels, and at the same time swing the arms upwards and overhead. Return to the original standing position and repeat. It is important in this exercise to switch the eyes upwards as the arms travel overhead, keeping your gaze glued on your thumbs until you assume the standing position again. Still standing, feet together, raise the left knee so that the thigh is horizontal, at the same time swinging the right arm to its fullest extent in an upright direction. Repeat the performance but reverse the limbs and carry on alternately, making sure to raise the opposite arm to the leg that is being raised. Follow this with a similar exercise, but instead of raising the knee kick the leg out straight in front of you and at the same time fling up the opposite arm. You will probably find other exercises that improve balance and the more you can vary them the better. But remember that all the time you are acquiring balance you are performing exercises that also have beneficial results so far as development of muscle and all-round agility is concerned.

So much for balance - now we come to aim, timing and power of punch. These three are developed simultaneously so we will take them together. To attain perfection we need the aid of a sparring partner, the use of the punch-ball, of which there are several different types, and a knowledge of shadow boxing. When sparring use the heavy, well-padded gloves in order that you can punch your hardest without risk of harming your partner. It is no use being kind to him by pulling your punches as you will soon drop into the habit and find it impossible to produce a knockout punch at the psychological moment. If you can get the help, spar with a man lighter than yourself in order to work up speed and take on a man who is heavier for the building-up of stamina and staying power.

Just at first you may find it is far from an easy matter to penetrate the defences of your sparring partners. But if you devote care and thought to the study of feinting - a sadly neglected art I regret to say - you will find that difficulties diminish. Always remember that your feet are as important elements in your success as your hands, and that by side-stepping, retiring and also by sudden and unexpected advances it is often quite possible to catch an opponent off his guard and then discover an easy way through. Watch your man

carefully, especially when you suspect him of an intention to attack. For then you can often surprise him with a swift time thrust (as it is styled in fencing).

This is one of the simplest and most effective punches. Feign a retreat in order to lure your opponent into a rush, then stop suddenly and shoot your left to his face. This will, in the majority of cases, be temporarily unguarded, since, if he is coming on filled with a desire to demolish you, he will generally dash in with either his hands down or as open as a barn door. In any event, *he* will be coming on towards *you* and at such a pace or with such energy that he will be unable to either side-step, swerve or duck out of the way of your delivery. Your left will consequently be far more likely to get home without interruption, especially if you have trained this weapon to obey your eye by careful practice in shadow boxing and with a punch-ball. Finally, your punch, when it arrives, should be distinctly effective. It cannot help being a forceful one, since it will carry with it, not only all the energy you have imparted to it personally, but also that with which your rival has generously contributed by the force of his own advance.

All of which brings me back to the second essential of the

straight left as the most valuable boxing asset, *viz.*, that after its accuracy has been carefully developed, the most careful attention should next be devoted to the development of its forceful delivery. Force is always the final argument in everything. The finest and most perfect strategy can affect little or indeed nothing without solid force to back it up and carry out its plans. So while we must concede to skill the pride of place in the armoury of boxing, skill alone will not win verdicts (and most certainly will fail to record knockout wins) unless this same skill is backed up by the power of the punches which it directs. But these punches should not, cannot indeed, properly derive their power from a wild exertion of the whole body. A punch need only travel a few inches to send even the strongest and toughest man crashing to the canvas, in fact, the very hardest punches which have ever been delivered in a contest have only been fully appreciated by the spectators by their visible result. They usually *seem* to be light, simple affairs, effortless to all appearance, and to a certain extent, almost effortless in actual fact, yet the recipients have had no doubts as to their destructive qualities. Summing it up, the whole secret of the actual force of a terrific punch is the accuracy of its timing, coordinated, of course, with the accuracy of its aim.

On the other hand, disastrous results can occur to the boxer who neglects timing and aim, as apart from the fact that the act of missing your target places you at a disadvantage straight away, it is a decidedly barren policy to endeavour to score points by hitting the empty air, due to the fact that when your punch arrives its objective has moved elsewhere. And even if you strike your target without perfect timing and perfect aiming you may find you have struck the top of his head instead of his face or caught his elbow instead of his mid-section, and as a result suffer not only a painful jar but possible injury. Just because you are engaged in sparring do not let yourself think for a single moment that you can slack up in your intensity of purpose. You must be just as determined as if you were fighting for your very existence, making every step and blow a scientific move and encouraging your sparring partner to act likewise, so that the whole of your workout has the appearance of the real thing.

The punch-ball, in its variety of patterns, is an essential part of a boxer's equipment, but here again you must be serious in your treatment of it and get to work with the intention of developing your timing and accuracy of aim, ignoring any tendency or inclination you may have to provide an exhibition for any onlookers that may happen to be in the gymnasium. For, I suppose, with the view of making sure of being able to punch the ball at all, and with a quite understandable desire to avoid making themselves look ridiculous to any casual spectators in their early ball-punching days, many boxers fall into the habit of "tapping" the swinging ball from close range. They stand up close to the ball and rarely, if ever, shift their position. Then, since it appears to them less difficult to hit the ball and to keep it swinging with a full round-arm swing or with semi-circular blows, it is no wonder that the novice finds himself acquiring the use of swings and hooks in his boxing, thus rendering the punch-ball useless as a means of perfecting the straight left.

Yet ball-punching practised as it should be practised, will do more to develop straight hitting perhaps than any other means. I would therefore strongly recommend the aspiring boxer to disregard criticism, either self-conscious or from onlookers. You are practising with the ball with a view to developing your boxing abilities and should firmly resolve to keep this main object in view. The punch-ball was invented for the primary purpose of developing a boxer's ability to hit both hard and straight. After all, it is easier to punch even a swinging ball than a dodging, ducking, side-stepping or dancing opponent. The range can be calculated with greater certainty and the ball is incapable of warding off or parrying the punches aimed at it.

Stand up to it, therefore, at about the distance you would

stand from an opponent whom you were facing in the ring and punch at it straight with the left hand. Practise punching it, with simple, straight leads, and practise no other style of punch until you are quite satisfied that you can hit it whenever and however you want so to do. Then, but not until then, vary your straight leads or jabs with right ones. Only make sure they are right crosses, that is to say, right-hand punches, which would in a contest, shoot over your opponent's left shoulder to his face. These being sent along a slight diagonal will vary the angle at which the ball comes back thus enabling you to develop an additional accuracy with your straight lefts, which can be shot home either alternately or in varying intermission with your right crosses. And, thereby, two punches have been mastered.

Once again let me warn you against all temptations to indulge in fancy work. Remember that you are not trying to become an exhibition ball-puncher, unless you have ambitions in that direction. But if you have you would be well advised to give up boxing. There have been men who could make a living either in the ring or as expert fancy ball punchers, but the two professions do not mix well as a rule. So cut out the fancy tricks just as you have already (as I hope you have) cut out all inclinations to regard your ball-punching exercises as a light and easy performance which you can run through in any old way. You may think fit to take three-minute spells at the ball. It is not a bad idea, but if you are going to treat these spells as rounds in time, why not go the further step and make them rounds in very essence, as far as it is possible to do so.

For example, do not be content with the ordinary method of tapping the ball and of interspersing your taps with occasional blows with your full strength. This system of exercise will admittedly develop your wind, staying power, hitting muscles and the power of your punch to some extent, but there are other exercises which will produce these results with greater benefit to yourself. Regard the punch-ball rather as

an aid to accuracy and straight hitting, not forgetting, of course, such punches as will develop your ability to hit forcibly from as many various angles and positions as you can imagine. Be very certain that it will be scarcely possible for you to imagine too many variations in this direction. For, in the course of a serious contest you may find yourself most curiously situated at times, and if you have trained yourself in the preservation of balance and the arts of accurate and forceful aim, no matter how placed, you will frequently he able to send home a surprise punch which may easily carry you a considerable distance along the path to victory.

Once you have acquired the knack of keeping the ball on the move, abandon your stationary post and learn how to *fight* the ball. Spar up to it as you would to an active opponent in the ring. Dance round it, advance, retire, dash past it, duck under it, uppercut it at times. Tap it now and then, of course, just as you would tap an opponent's guard in the course of feinting. Hook at times; in fact, hook frequently, in order to develop the force of this useful punch - which is really only a variant of the straight left and not a bent arm blow as imagined by the uninitiated - but as a general rule, when hitting out with your left from any distance, school yourself into the habit of hitting straight. Cross your right or hook with the right, and then practice the knack of delivering straight lefts from the edgewise classical position, at the diagonal crossing ball. But above all, *never swing at the ball.*

If by any chance a punch-ball is not available, either the platform ball, the suspended ball or the spring-ball, use a small bag filled with peas and suspended from a rafter - you don't need a heavy punch-sack until you come to practise straight left drives to the body. Another idea is to use a length of half-inch rope, strung from a rafter, with a knot in the end. This does not, of course, help to develop punching power, like the punch-ball or sack, but it is a wonderful way of perfecting aim. Dance round it as it swings to and fro and pepper it with fast straight lefts, trying hard to hit the knot with every delivery. When performing on the punch-ball or sack you will use bandaged hands or punching gloves, but with the swinging rope use the bare fists.

In shadow-boxing, which is usually performed in the most lackadaisical fashion by the average boxer in training, try your hardest to make this resemble an actual contest as closely as you possibly can. Don't just move round, sparring, feinting and hitting at nothing, simply and solely for the sake of exercise as so many boxers do. This popular method has its uses, of course, but it can be easily rendered far more useful than it usually is. Another thing, don't carry out your shadow boxing and at the same time hold a running commentary with an admirer who may be watching you. Keep your mind on the job, imagine that your worst enemy, if you happen to have one, is there in front of you and go out to give him all you have got. Use your imagination to the utmost, try and anticipate the moves your  phantom rival will endeavour to put across and work yourself up into a real fighting frame of mind. And do not give an exhibition of fancy stuff but while using every punch in your repertoire be sure to make the straight left predominate.

If you cannot do your shadow-boxing in a ring, mark out on the floor of your gymnasium or training room a square the exact size of a ring and use every inch of the space. Start from one corner and advance diagonally across the ring to the opposite corner, deliver straight left punches on the way. Pursue this path back and forth several times in succession, going in for a spell of speedy in-fighting when reaching a corner, but in mid-ring and during your progress from one corner to another, practise solely the straight left and guard. Then suddenly switch to other punches, practising the left lead and right cross, left lead and right uppercut, left to head and left to body, and so on. But for a period of at least two rounds make the straight left lead a regular first, no matter how you might vary the movements of the right hand.

CHAPTER FIVE
THE STRAIGHT LEFT IN DEFENCE

In the recording of points scored, by which referees are solely justified in the rendering of their decisions, preference is, or invariably should be, given to "attack". It is true that points are also recorded for skill in defence and for style, etc., but the chief stress is laid on attack. Successful attack, be it remembered - a point which the majority of average spectators, and which, I am sorry to have to say, some referees are apt to forget. No boxer should ever be credited, for any merits they may imagine they have earned for useless, unprofitable pursuit, no matter how persistent. Yet you sometimes find verdicts given amid volumes of applause to men who have simply charged and kept on charging throughout a contest, who have kept up a perpetual rain of blows at their opponents, but who have failed to send home more than a very small percentage of these to the only targets which the rules of boxing recognise, and who, so far as points actually scored are concerned (that is to say, in the form of clean hits delivered with the knuckle part of the gloves on the front and sides of their opponent's head or body) are actually badly in arrears at the close.

Unfortunately, in these instances both the referee and the spectators have permitted themselves to be led astray by the fire and fury of the attacks, which have over-shadowed in their minds their ill-success. They have seen that one of the contestants was forced mainly to retreat, and noting this they failed to notice that he was really fighting a series of skillful rearguard actions, that he was continually "pinking" his rushing antagonist, and, in fact, generally accumulating a highly respectable score of points. Such a case as this is of course distinctly rough on the better boxer, and at times may have its influence on his subsequent career. He may come to the conclusion that there is very little, if anything, to be gained by the study or practice of skillful boxing, and he may consequently wander away into the rushing, swinging path himself.

Yet, although he is entitled to sympathy for his unmerited misfortune, he is nevertheless largely to blame for it. No referee is infallible, and there are and always will be officials who are unable to resist the contagion of popular enthusiasm. The referee may firmly resolve that he will render an absolutely impartial verdict. He may even think that he has done so - and yet it may happen that the verdict has actually been given by the partisan sympathies of the spectators. There may have been many interested in the fortunes of a favourite. They may have been so desperately anxious to see him returned as victor as to obscure their vision of the feats of his opponent. In the ordinary phrase, they can only see their own man; with the result that believing the desires of their hearts, they not only satisfy themselves that he has won, but actually succeed in hypnotising the referee into a similar frame of mind. These things are all in the luck of the game and should not only be recognised, but also allowed for, by every boxer.

We all have to fall back at times, in fact, it is quite possible to win contests by merely ducking, dodging, side-stepping, feinting and dancing away. It might also be said that it is possible to win a knockout victory over a certain class of opponents without placing a glove on them. This, of course, is actually an exaggeration of fact, though a perfectly correct statement in all other essentials. My actual meaning is that by a process of continual dodging and by thereby forcing your opponent to repeated misses and other abortive attacks, you can reduce him to such a state of exhaustion that he will collapse through sheer loss of wind and stamina. You take him out of his stride, make him travel and keep him travelling at a much faster pace than any to which he is accustomed or trained, and in such a case neither his organs nor will-power can possibly withstand the strain. Against this it might be argued that you will yourself be in an equally evil case, but such is very far from the probabilities, if one only plays the game as it should be played. For the man who attacks and misses, takes far more out of himself than the man who is content merely to avoid.

But in actual practice, of course, the man who is playing the defensive game should vary his policy of "getting away" by frequent introduction of the "stop" policy. By this I do not mean the "stop" in ordinary acceptance of the term, which implies the parry or guard, or even the other and more valuable method of stopping which results from a well-applied and timely push to your opponent's arm or shoulder. The "stop" with which I am now dealing is that applied by a stiff, straight left jab. Even when you and your opponent are practically stationary, that is to say, are not dancing about, but are merely employing eye feints or those other "draws" for a lead, which consist in threatening movements of the hands and arms, not forgetting leg and foot shuffles, you can frequently slip in a sudden and disconcerting jab to the other fellow's face at the very moment when he is about to let go a real punch at you.

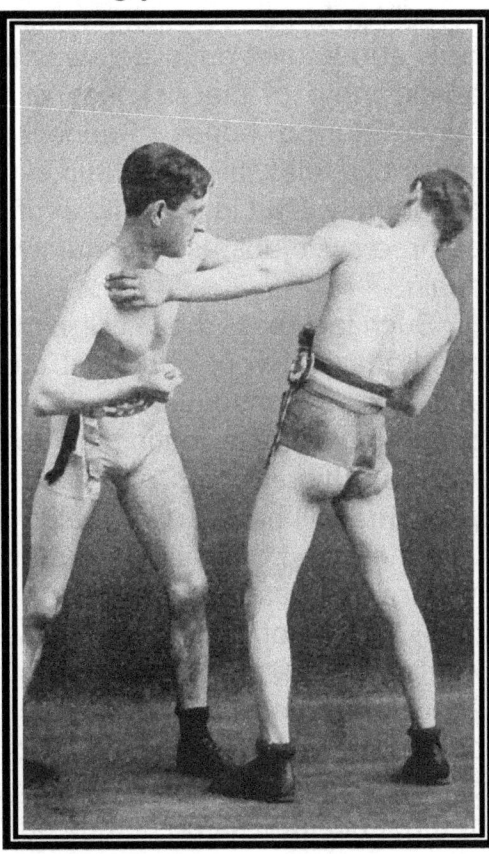

You will then have "beaten him to the punch", as the phrase goes. In other words, you will have coaxed him into starting a punch, but will have met him with your own after he has committed himself to his, but before he can get his home, which can only be done by the exercise of the most accurate judgment of time and distance. But perhaps the most effective defensive straight left-handed "stop" is that which is, or should be employed, against the determined rushes or persistently attacking opponent. For these men are really, after all, the easiest men in the world to beat at the boxing game.

With a certain class of opponent, I might almost say with every brand of opponent you are likely to meet, it is always best to coax them into as much attacking as you can. For it stands to reason that the man who has committed himself to a serious attack has thereby inevitably weakened his powers of defence. He has deprived himself both of the power and ability to recover himself, that is to say, to change directly from attack to defence. Hence the advantages which will accrue to the boxer who has carefully studied and practised the retreating game. One can draw this class of man after one, build him up with hopes that he is going to get you "cornered", or force you back against the ropes, and then, just as he is about to let go, slide away from him and leave him with a little more of the sickness of heart which always comes from deferred hopes. Sooner or later he will, he must, inevitably relax his watchfulness and then will come your opportunity. Dart in like a flash of lightning, deal out one, two, or three swift jabs as opportunity occurs, and then dart away again.

Such tactics as these will in ninety-nine cases out of every hundred bring your opponent charging after you again, and as a natural consequence present you with numerous other opportunities for repeating the dose - until you can plainly see that both his strength and wind have nearly left him, when your time will have arrived to go in and finish him off. A very useful method of forcing the man you meet into these rushing and persistent onslaughts - the simplest and surest, in fact - is that of a gradual but steady retreat to commence with. Fall back steadily as the other man comes on, and at about the same pace. But check him as he advances with occasional left jabs. These should, indeed, must be, stiff punches delivered with a straight arm. Let the arm shoot out to meet his face as he comes on, but be careful to avoid any preliminary "pull-back" of the arm, shoulder or elbow, before you thrust. Take all the driving power you may require from your legs and back. Remember that the punch must be a snappy one, if it is to be really effective, but remember at the same time that it will gain a very appreciable amount of its force from the pace at which the recipient is coming to meet it.

But first, last, and all the time, be particularly careful that you *always* get home with these jabs. For serious trouble, if not disaster, will almost inevitably be the penalty you will pay for missing. Yes, I know quite well that it is easier to miss than to hit, but then it is really easier to hit than it is to miss with the blows I am describing. For if you are falling back correctly, are conducting your retreat at precisely the right pace, and are careful to keep your balance perfect, you should experience little difficulty either in selecting your opportunities or in making sure of your aim. You ought to have the distance measured to a fraction of an inch. It should not be difficult to accurately judge the pace at which the other fellow is coming towards you, and then, since you will seize an opportunity when you are reasonably certain that your opponent is just starting a punch at you, you will have been presented with a practically open target. For in order to hit you he must necessarily uncover his face. There will, of course, be occasions when he will keep this protected, but on those you will wisely refrain from even thinking of a time jab, and continue your retreat.

In case you should accuse me of having failed to cover the whole subject, you can rest assured if you are retreating and your pursuer has really made up his mind to attack with all his force, that he will make a final leap to do so. This will, of course, be necessary if he is hoping to cover the space you will have preserved between you. It will also render him more open to your jab, by the way. So that all you need do is to stop short in your retreat, shoot out a straight, absolutely stiff arm and wrist and receive his nose or mouth on the end, the knuckle part, of your left glove. The faster and more vigorous his leap, the bigger the shock which he will receive. It may even happen that you will then be able to see your way clear to a quick finish, or at least to the administration of severe punishment. In any case, you will be able to congratulate yourself on having taken a good deal of the steam out of your man with that one punch, and in almost every one that you deliver, and will be well able to extract a good deal more by the delivery of two or three additional ones before you break away to resume operations. Indeed, the only fly in your ointment will be that you will have given your opponent a very shrewd warning as to the sort of fate which will await him if he rushes again, and that you will consequently have to work hard before you can persuade him to rush again.

To conclude this chapter of "Defence", let me once again stress the importance of acquiring the art of "milling on the retreat". Practise shooting out a straight left while you back away round the ring, but be sure to make certain that you do not allow yourself to be trapped in a corner. Even in this unenviable position it is possible to extricate yourself without having had to suffer damage, simply by keeping the left going in accurate manner as you swerve and sway out of danger, until the moment arrives when you can slip away altogether. No matter how hard you may be pressed by a determined attacker, never be tempted to forsake straight hitting for round-arm blows and never be misguided enough to wade in and swap punches in haphazard fashion. Put all your trust in well-placed, hard-driven, left shots to the head and body and very soon you will find the storm abating as your accurate punching begins to take effect.

Apart from using the straight left as a counter to any blow your opponent may endeavour to send over, and apart also from any skill you may possess in the avoidance of a damaging punch, either by ducking, side-stepping, drawing back or swerving, always remember that feinting is just as good a means of defending oneself as it is an asset in attacking. If you are being heavily attacked and forced to give ground make it appear every now and again that you are about to launch a vigorous counterattack or that, in desperation, you are going to put all you have got into a determined blow with which you hope to check the assault you are undergoing. Give your rival the feint, then instead of carrying out your threat, pop him neatly on the nose with a hard straight left or dig him in the mid-section below his guard. One or two moves like this will soon shatter his confidence and so turn the tide of battle.

CHAPTER SIX
STRAIGHT LEFT IN ATTACK

I have already stated that attack is the trump suit in boxing, and have also pointed out that attack does not necessarily mean rushing or charging at or after your opponent. Attack, indeed, commences earlier than hitting. For the ideal punch, or perhaps it would be better to say the best punch, the most effective one, is a good stiff counter to a ducked, brushed-aside, or otherwise evaded lead. It is usually best, whenever possible, to "draw" your opponent into a lead before hitting out on your own account. The advantages gained thereby are four in number. In the first place, you have forced your opponent to commit himself to a decided step and can therefore be moderately certain of what he is about to do. Secondly, you have to a very large extent deprived him of the ability to change his position and guard swiftly enough to deal successfully with any offensive you may yourself adopt. Thirdly, by his mere action of hitting out, you will or should secure an opening of sorts, can or should make him present you with a fair target at which to aim. Fourthly, and most important of all, you will have borrowed some very considerable force from him to add to the power of your own "counter" delivery. For the more speedy and the heavier his advance or lunge towards you in the action of punching, the heavier and more painful will be the "dig" with which you meet him on his way.

In the normal course of instruction in the boxing gymnasium, the pupil is almost invariably taught that the most I effective reply to the left lead is that known as "the right cross counter", partly because it looks so much more in accordance with the fitness of things, but mainly, I suspect, because when all is said and done the right cross counter, effectively and properly planted on the jaw, will almost invariably finish a contest there and then. But, just because it is the normal reply to the left lead, the majority of boxers are usually careful to keep a watchful eye open for it, and for that very reason it is one of the most difficult punches to land just when one wants to place it where it will do most good.

Nevertheless, it is sometimes a sound policy to try the effect of one right at the start of a contest. A good deal will depend on your man. But if you are able to feint skillfully and have thereby succeeded in "drawing" your opponent into attempting a really forceful lead, you will not infrequently be able to glimpse an opening for the right cross. If and when you do, be always careful to let it go good and hard with all your might.

You may remember that quite a number of even important ring battles, even championship battles, too, at that, have been won and lost by what was practically the first punch delivered. Also that in nearly every one of these cases it was a good right cross which did the trick. Yes, the right cross may often be sent home at the very start of a contest when it would be useless to attempt it against a really good man again for many a weary round. So very few really good boxers are liable to expect that their opponents will venture to attempt such a cheeky proceeding right at the start. And in boxing it is the unexpected which happens more frequently than anything else.

But this is supposed to be a treatise on the use of the left hand, and the above is consequently a digression from the path. I would ask you to bear the right cross in mind, but to rely mainly on left-hand countering as an attacking blow. Never neglect any single opportunity of improving yourself in the art of "beating your opponent to the punch". Get your sparring partners to start punches first of all. Specified punches, if you prefer, but secondly and principally, unexpected punches, and then try to beat them both in time and pace. Set up as your motto, "I will get there first". Because if you can get the man in front of you to start the punch and can be sure of sending your counter home first, you cannot only rest assured that you will get home ever so much harder, but you will also be relieved of all the worries attaching to the necessities of either guard or evasion. You may sometimes, indeed, frequently, be able to land a most effective wallop

after you have brushed an opponent's lead to one side, because in so doing you will inevitably disturb his balance and thereby render an upset more possible. But as a general rule, you will find circumstances better adapted to the counter direct and simple.

Ducking, side-stepping, or parrying will almost invariably distract the concentration of your thoughts, and consequently diminish the force of your own punch, if only because your duck, side-step or parry may have presented the other fellow with an opportunity for self-recovery - while in addition he will not in such case be in full momentum. His lunge forward accompanying his punch will have almost, if not quite, finished, and you will then have very little additional force to borrow from him. I may add from practical experience that the average tear-away fighter, who is so fond of rushing in at his opponents with the intent to sweep them off the face of the earth, can generally be brought up short in mid-career and very effectually disgruntled by a series of swift, stiff, stabs to the face. It is usually necessary to break ground before him for a time, and the man who hesitates to break ground where the occasion demands, simply and solely for the look of the thing, does not deserve to succeed. In boxing, the feet are every whit as important as the hands. Use them. Get in and get out again, but be careful always if possible to land a telling jab every time you do get in.

Pretty nearly every man who cares to do so can develop a highly respectable left-hand dig. A good deal will of course depend on his natural gifts. But it is by no means always the big hefty fellow who hits the hardest. The vast majority of boxers weary themselves with appliances and special exercises in order to develop their hitting powers. Some swear by the sandbag, others devote hours to swinging at a ball. Some try hand-balances, ground exercises, or heavy wall machines, and thereby tighten up their muscles, losing speed in the process and incidentally hitting power itself. For big punches do not come from big muscles, it is the long, supple muscles that carry real kick. The whole secret of hard hitting lies in accurate timing and in mental application. Make up your mind that you will hit as hard as you possibly can, with every ounce of your bodily strength, and above all, with every fibre of your mental determination, and also that you will keep hitting harder and harder as you progress and you can rest assured that your hitting powers will develop rapidly. Remember that you must take up power from the ground through your legs and your back.

When it comes to setting up an attack, lead off with a swift straight left, either to the head or body - it all depends where you perceive an opening or feel you can force one - and if you reach your target do not stand back and admire your handiwork, but send home another blow to the same point. Let one blow follow the other with rapidity, making a "double punch" of it and the damaging psychological effect is unmistakable. But let each punch be full of ginger-not mere taps that look good, but honest-to-goodness jabs that really jar. Should your opponent raise his guard in an effort to prevent you reaching his face again, immediately drive in a straight punch to the body and switch from one objective to the other, each time he puts up a cover. All the while, keep advancing, left foot gliding forward and stepping up quickly with the right.

If you find that your rival is effectively guarding against or blocking every punch you try at his face and is equally good at protecting his body when you switch downstairs, aim at his left biceps until he presents you with another opening to a vulnerable spot. The continuous pounding of his biceps will have the effect of making it difficult for him to lift his arm after a few rounds and then you can score to the face as and when you please. Remember that speed is essential, not only in attack, but in every phase of boxing. Once you have got him on the defensive, keep him there. Never let up in your assault, keep it going methodically, but all the time slightly increasing the pace so that he gets no respite whatsoever.

But when once you have got him in trouble do not lose your head and start swinging in an effort to finish him off. Bring the right into play by all means, but keep punching straight and true. More than one boxer has been within an inch of winning a contest, but has thrown the fight away by foolishly losing control and starting to swing wildly from all angles in the hopes of bringing off a spectacular victory. His wild punches have been much easier to avoid and moreover there is a great possibility that his "half-beaten" opponent has merely been "foxing" or feigning weakness and distress and suddenly comes back with a heavy punch that crashes through the lost defence with devastating results.

Take my advice and leave swinging alone if you have any ambition at all to reach the heights in boxing. In the first place it is far easier to miss with a swinging punch than with a straight delivery, and in the second, the results of missing may easily be disastrous. If you miss with a huge swing, or "haymaker" as the Americans term it, you are practically certain to become unbalanced and consequently at the mercy of your opponent. If, on the other hand, the miss happens to be only partial, that is to say, a miss with the glove and not with the arm, the odds are that the blow will be delivered incorrectly (*i.e.*, not with the knuckle part of the hand), in which case the puncher is liable to be more severely hurt than his opponent. He may even break his hand, and thereby practically destroy all his chances, not only of victory, but of a prolonged career in the ring. The big swing which goes hurtling through the air, and which looks such a terribly devastating affair, can in any case only carry with it the force of the deliverer. There is all the difference in the results which exist between the striking of a motionless cricket ball or the kicking of a motionless football and the striking or kicking of one which rapidly is coming towards one.

I may add that the swing has even another and greater disadvantage than this. For, since, in order to swing, a man must necessarily make his arm traverse a fairly lengthy arc in the air, he can scarcely fail to convey some intimation of the blow intended, and that warning may and probably will be sufficiently far forward to cause the swing to miss altogether, either by passing behind or around the neck of the intended recipient, or else over his head, and consequently resulting in a sheer waste of energy without the disturbance of anything except the atmosphere. And even supposing that the swerving head has not moved sufficiently out of range to escape

actual contact, the punch, when it does land, will in most cases only succeed in striking a target which is moving away - and it is surely scarcely necessary for me to point out that a blow of this kind is most unlikely to prove very effective.

Heavy swings, which get "home" are frequently very effective, but I am prepared to maintain - and have proved by physical demonstrations - that they can never be relied upon for accuracy of aim. Nor can they ever be proved to be harder blows or even as hard as the correct straight delivery. They only look heavier. Of course, I have myself swung, at times. Every man who wants to mount high in the boxing profession will have perforce to pay some little attention to this department of hitting. For variety in style, method, tactics and strategy is one of the prime elements of success. I would like to lay it down as a golden rule for all ambitious boxers, that they should never swing - except when occasion demands. For instance, it is sometimes useful or rather may be profitable to let go a few swings and even a few apparently wild ones, for strategic purposes and with a view of suggesting both to

one's opponent and to his advisors in his corner that one is mentally worried and even possibly in physical distress.

Again, occasions will frequently arise when it will be possible to land a swinging punch only. (For you will remember that I laid stress on the necessity for practicing the art of hitting from every conceivable angle and from every possibly imaginable position.) Say that your opponent is covered up, that is to say, that he has missed you, or that you have side-stepped his attack and that he is consequently going past you. He has smothered his face and head with his gloves and protected his ribs with his elbows and forearms. In such a position, you may be presented with a splendid opportunity for delivering a swing to the ribs or by pushing aside his defence, a hook to the head, or even an uppercut to the chin. But there will be other occasions when you may be able to cause him more pain and to thereby secure a better advantage for yourself, by the delivery of an upward swinging blow to the pit of his stomach. Yet all these are but the exceptions which are proverbially said to prove the rule, that straight punches are and always will be far more effective in the long run than any swinging deliveries.

CHAPTER SEVEN
COUNTERING THE STRAIGHT LEFT

No matter how proficient you may become in the use of the straight left there will inevitably be times in your fistic career when you must come up against an opponent who is, if not your superior, at least your equal in the practice of the premier weapon. He might have brought his use of the blow to the tiniest degree nearer a state of perfection than yourself or, and this is a far more likely proposition, he may have physical advantages - increased width of shoulders, height and corresponding reach - which enables him to beat you to the punch. In these cases, your skill in attack and cleverness in defence may not be sufficient, so I am devoting my last chapter of instruction to the ways and means by which a superior exponent of the straight left may have his work nullified or be countered and so punished that the advantages with which he opened the contest are slowly but surely reduced in value until matters become on a more equal footing. Take heed, however, and realise that these very methods of countering a straight left boxer will be used against yourself, so you must be ever watchful for them in order that you are not taken unawares.

First, we will deal with the straight left to the head. This can be avoided, by swaying sufficiently to the right so that your opponent's left glove passes harmlessly over your left shoulder. Try this move and you will at once see that by making him miss in this way you are in an ideal position to drive home a countering left to the body or else a damaging right hook to the heart.

Another method is to catch the attacking left arm with your right glove and push it away to your left. This has the effect of putting him off balance and completely at your mercy for the delivery of a countering blow with the left.

Once more your rival leads off with a straight left to the head. This time sway away from the blow to the right, thus moving "inside" the punch. Here again you have an excellent opening for a countering stroke - a hard right-handed drive to the body which by reason of your body movement can be sent home with a maximum of power.

Or, sway away slightly to the right, allowing your opponent's left lead to pass over your shoulder and with the same movement bang home your own straight left to his jaw. Again, it will be appreciated that the act of swaying will automatically put more striking power behind your own delivery and this is one of the most effective counters to a left lead, especially if your opponent has the advantage of a longer reach.

I have already advised pushing away your opponent's arm to the right, but this move can be varied by knocking up the intended blow and sending home your own left to the midsection. It is, however, much easier to brush the arm aside than to knock it up and my only reason for mentioning this alternative method is for the simple fact that it is as well to have a change in tactics, otherwise your rival will soon get the hang of your moves and plan his campaign accordingly and to your detriment. Do not attempt to brush his left lead away to the right as this will turn him in your direction and should he plan a countering right to the body or head it will, of course, carry extra power in its course.

We now come to the right cross, in other words, the straight right counter to the left lead which crosses over the striking arm of your opponent and catches him on the side of the jaw. It is, if properly delivered and accurately timed, a shattering blow and very often has decisive results. But it requires extensive practice to bring it to perfection. First of all, you must "draw" your opponent's lead and avoid its impact by withdrawing your head a matter of inches, at the same time coming up on the ball of your right foot and shooting your right hard across his left shoulder to the jaw. Your delivery will either be a definite straight right or you may have to hook the blow, giving it that last moment twist in order to plant your back knuckles solidly upon their objective.

My own specialty in the way of a counter to a left lead to the head is known as the "inside parry". Instead of drawing the lead and countering with a right cross to the jaw, sway

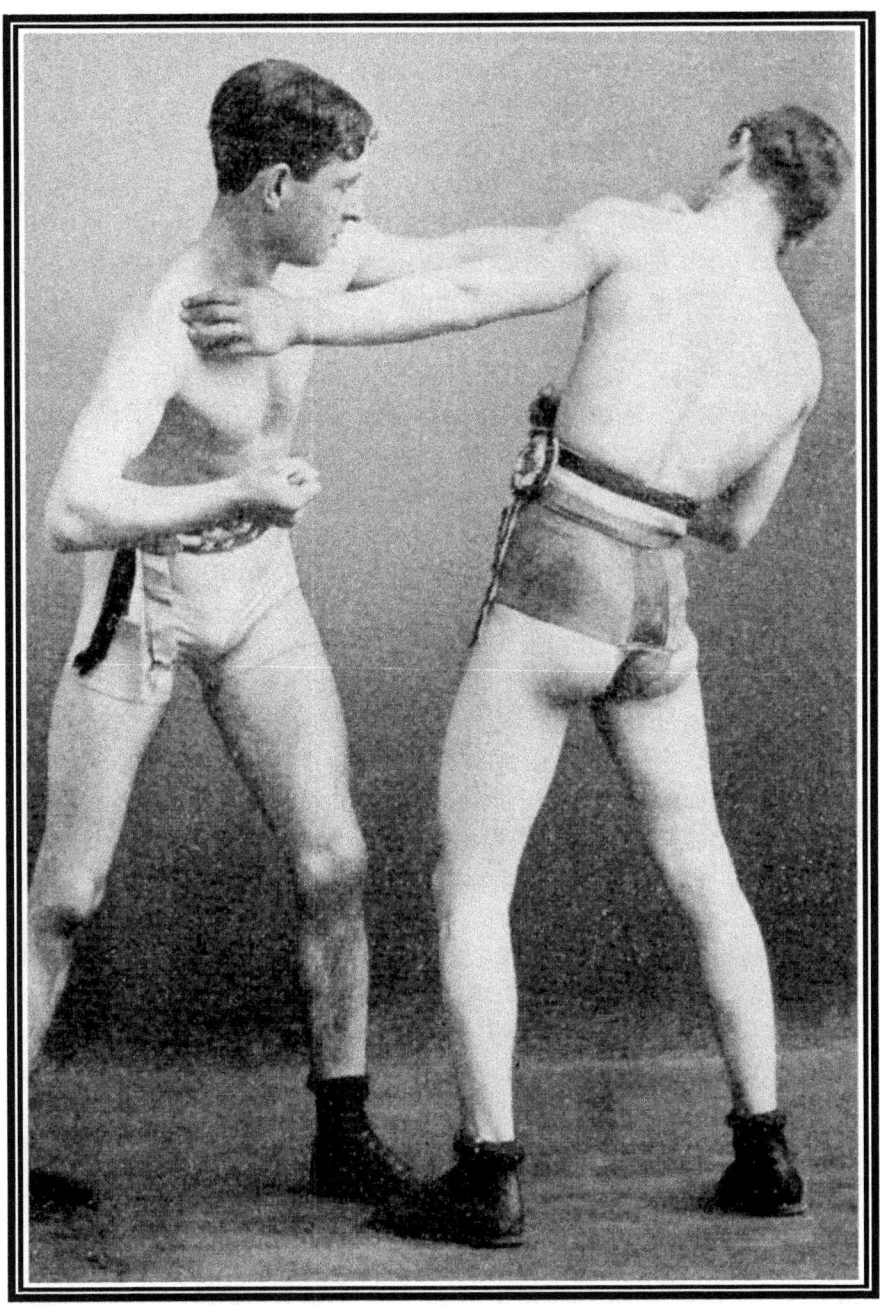

slightly to the left and drive the right "inside" your opponent's striking arm to catch him on the jaw with a solid, shaking blow. Let me stress, however, that again this is a delivery that demands accurate aiming and timing and one you must practice assiduously if you are to bring it off successfully.

Another very effective counter to a straight left lead is the countering left. With this move you do not sway either to left or right, but merely withdraw the head an inch or so in order to make your rival fall short with his delivery. You then come back immediately with a straight left drive to the head. This usually comes as a distinct surprise to your opponent who having been intent on scoring himself, finds that he has been the receiver instead and to his chagrin, caught by the very blow that he had planned to deliver. The main counter to a straight left drive to the mid-section is of course the right cross to the jaw, but in this instance it must of necessity be delivered in a downwards direction, as in launching his own blow your opponent must automatically bend forward. But with this particular attack it is best to go on the defensive, i.e., rather than take a blow in the hopes of landing an effective counter, do not take the blow at all. The guard for a left drive to the body is the left elbow which is pressed firmly against your own body as an intervening shield. Not only is it desirable to avoid damage to the mid-section, but the elbow provides a very bony obstruction and your rival will not risk bruising his knuckles very often.

Always make a point of using your other arm as a shield when either leading or countering. When using the left keep the right arm raised with the glove protecting the face and your elbow guarding your body; the same applies to the left arm when countering with your right. This is of vital importance for it is of no use perfecting your own hitting, both in accuracy and power, if you are not also equipped with the moves with which to guard against the blows delivered by a rival. Never drop your hands to your sides - you have a full minute to rest them in at the end of each round - and if you lower them during the course of action you will find it difficult to raise them quickly again in order to ward off another attack. Apart from that you will be expending energy unnecessarily and you can take it from me that in no contest of any seriousness will you have energy to spare.

ADDENDUM

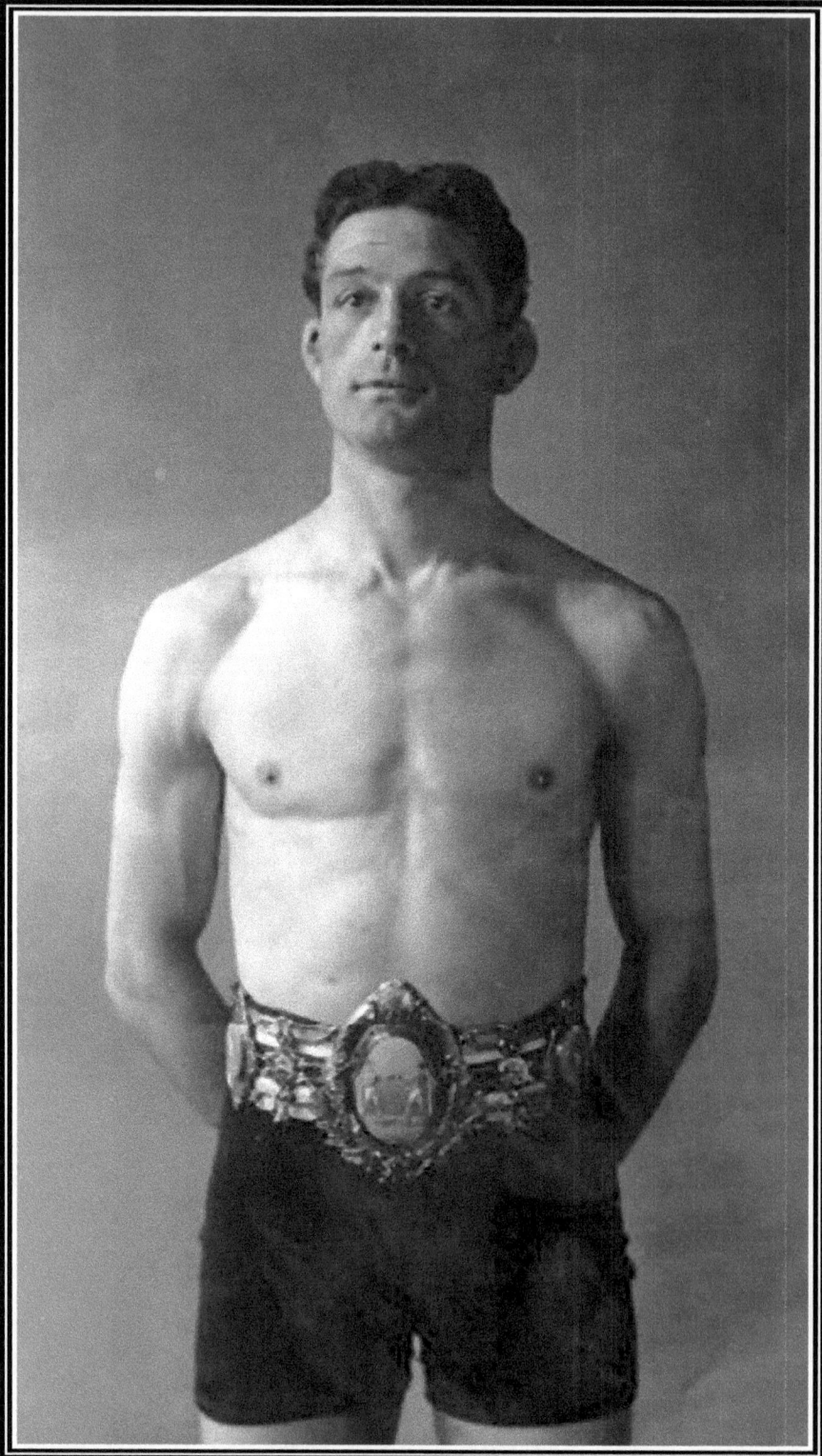

Peerless Jim
Life and Fights of Jim Driscoll

By Gilbert E. Odd

There have perhaps been greater boxers than Jim Driscoll, but, with the sole exception of the Australian marvel, Young Griffo, confirmatory evidence of such superiority, if any, is not forthcoming. Driscoll, famed in this country and in the United States as "Peerless Jim", stood out from the crowd as the one classic model, the truly scientific boxer, who had not only perfected every move in the game, but whose every move was precisely calculated, selected and timed. One has to suppose that there must have been a fair-sized foundation of native ability, for Jim first attracted notice at the age of fifteen or thereabouts, when he was employed in the machine-room of a newspaper office at Cardiff. Boxing was exceedingly popular among the boys there and a club was formed of which Driscoll not only became champion in short time, but also the idolised leader of the members. Not having the funds with which to buy gloves, the boys used waste paper from the reels and tied it on their hands. And that was the start of a great boxer's career.

There was no Welsh Amateur Boxing Association in those days, but local enthusiasts took it upon themselves to present trophies as a means of encouraging the lads and Driscoll won the majority of them. The acquisition of these "pots" was a secondary consideration, for Jim was out to embrace the "Noble Art of Self-Defence" in its entirety, otherwise the fact that one hard-earned "silver" cup promptly melted on the kitchen mantelpiece, might have had consequences serious to the sport of boxing.

Driscoll had brains, a far larger supply than most, and there is no doubt that he eventually took to the booth as a school, emerging as a perfected artist, if perfected by his own tuition and intuition. His title to fame, if possibly only to be preserved in boxing memory, rested mainly on a far wider basis. Certainly no other member of his profession has been, or is likely to be, so loved, one might almost say worshipped. He was literally the "King of Cardiff " and usually the outstanding figure of any and every group or circle in which he might find himself.

Few men have been trusted so implicitly, or have been so worthy of trust. His word was definitely his bond and it is the fact that promoters and others qualified to be judges of character were invariably content with a simple verbal promise from Jim, however resolute in their insistence on signatures, seals, or sworn and attested statements from others. Once Driscoll had passed his word those who dealt with him could rest content. Millions in bribes would be inadequate as compensation for any breach of his faith.

On one never-to-be-forgotten occasion, when in America and besieged with the most tempting offers, he steadfastly refused, simply and solely because he had promised to box at a charity tournament in his home town without recompense of any kind and possibly at no inconsiderable cost to himself. Nor was he solely the slave of his own word. Sovereign, by tacit consent, over the majority of South Welsh boxers and sportsmen generally, he could be safely relied upon to see that these also should and must live up to their verbal engagements and ever to "do the decent thing" when occasion arose. In that sense he was truly a monarch, an absolute king and one to be envied. Not only was the trust reposed in him absolute, but his judgment and settlement of any disputes which might occur was invariably sought and as invariably accepted without demur.

He had character, real strength of personality and, perhaps best asset of all, a limitless fund of humour. He had also

a turn of wit, sufficient to inspire an element of fear, but so singularly restrained that not even deeply pierced victims would ever nurse resentment. Jim would pull their legs unmercifully, until they were on the verge of boiling over and then switch them round to join in the general laughter.

His life in general must have been a very happy one, despite the prolonged internal trouble, gastric ulcers, which finally carried him off at the age of forty-five. Despite also certain financial ups and downs, he made money, not nearly so much as he could and would have made, had he made a more profound study of his own interests. But then he was a really lavish spender - on others. He did not give publicly, save of his services, and he was prodigal of these. On the other hand, he was continually dipping into his pocket to ease the needs of cases of real distress which came under his notice. These would often be thrust before him. He had but to show his face in London, at a boxing hall, to find a crowd waiting for him outside. The majority of these it is true were there to give vent to enthusiasm, but a definite percentage appeared in the hopes - and not vainly - of some monetary or other assistance.

He would not have been the great fistic master he was if he had not been such a sound and acute judge of character and individual peculiarities. He would own that while he had a reason for his every punch, or evasion, he could also when he chose, generally make his opponents beat themselves. For example, after one of his "Belt" fights, Driscoll remarked that he could have scored a knockout win, without having struck a really decisive blow. All he need have done, so he said, was to lure the other fellow on, to punch the air, until he fell exhausted. And, it has to be noted that the other fellow in question was a quite formidable puncher and a skillful and experienced boxer.

Jim knew the boxing game so thoroughly, that he knew he could never know it all. He owned, even towards the close of his generally triumphant career that he was still learning the art. He was such an ardent student that few acquaintances cared to  be in any close proximity when Driscoll was watching a contest as a spectator. His interest and self-identification was so keen that he would pantomime the punches which one of the actual contestants should have been shooting out and - well, some neighbour, whose presence he had forgotten, might find himself the
unhappy target.

Driscoll was twenty before he really turned professional fighting man. His first recorded contest is dated early in 1901, but he was a fully-fledged "pro" by that time, having taken part in scores of battles in the booths. He owed a lot at the start to Bob Downey, then a licensee in the heart of the Cardiff district known as "Niggertown", who took him under his wing and provided Jim with training quarters. Most of his sparring partners in those early days were coloured men, for Downey was a great friend to the coloured seamen. But as

Driscoll improved so he attracted other aspiring white boxers into his circle and very soon there existed a little camp of talented and ambitious boys. A Mr. Albert Shirley next interested himself as manager and backer and the whole company provided Jim with the very background and encouragement he needed.

Not that I do not believe he would have gone to the top of the tree alone and unaided, for Driscoll was a glutton for training and was determined to make good. He would go through a strenuous workout in the gymnasium and finish up by walking round the place on his hands, while he firmly believed in roadwork and never missed a daily spell of this gruelling and uninspiring exercise. Yet all through his training he remained the life and soul of the party, cheerful and joking, yet going through his routines with the utmost purpose and intent. Such enthusiasm, added to his natural talent, brought him along by leaps and bounds, and in a short time Professor Frank Cullis was seeking his services in his boxing booth. His two mentors were not averse to this, although they continued to look after Jim's interests from the commercial standpoint. So, for several years he fought under canvas, taking on all comers and fast picking up every move and artifice of the game. He performed in most of the principal Welsh towns and in such neighbouring places as Bristol, but it was not until 1904 that he made his debut in London.

The management at the National Sporting Club made it a rule to give opportunities to any provincial boxer with any show of talent and Driscoll was tried against a tough warrior by the name of "Boss" Edwards. The Welshman won readily enough on points after ten rounds and his style so impressed the members that he was up again before the year was out, this time in opposition to the formidable Johnny Summers. This contest, however, proved disappointing as the Londoner was disqualified in the second round, before the pair had really had time to properly test their mettle. In 1905 Jim won three further contests against fighters of repute and he was back at the National Sporting Club again in February of the following year, this time opposed to Jack Roberts, of Drury Lane, famed for his durability and aggressiveness. The Londoner put up a characteristic exhibition but he was outspeeded by the clever Cardiff lad, who cut him to ribbons with his accurate straight-left punching and battered him so badly that the referee called a halt to the proceedings in the seventh round and awarded the fight to Driscoll.

Three months later, Jim was again on view at "headquarters" taking part in the most important fight of his career. He had originally been engaged to tight a return contest with Summers, but the latter had to cry off through breaking down in training, and Joe Bowker, the bantamweight champion, was induced to meet the talented newcomer from Wales. As Bowker was short of training the contest was limited to fifteen rounds and it went its distance, with Driscoll a good winner on points. Twice during a hard-fought battle the title-holder was sent to the canvas, and it said a lot for his gameness that he was on his feet at the finish.

Just over a year later, on June 3, 1907, they met in a return contest, this time over the full championship distance of twenty rounds. The fight meant a tremendous lot to Jim, who was anxious to win and secure the winning end of the purse because he was set on getting married.

This time Bowker had no excuses to offer and entered the ring as fit as the proverbial fiddle. So well did he shape in the opening rounds that Driscoll boxed very carefully indeed, and left the majority of the forcing to his rival. Both men were putting up a delightful exhibition of pure boxing and it seemed that the contest would surely go the distance and it would be left for the referee to decide the winner. Then something happened.

One of Driscoll's supporters, anxious that Jim should make sure of victory, went round to his corner at the conclusion of the sixteenth round. "Jim," he whispered, "I have just heard that you will have to knock him out to win!"

"Well, I'll do it this round," was the calm reply. And true enough Bowker was counted out in the seventeenth round and Jim returned to Cardiff triumphantly to marry Miss Edith Wiltshire, whose father kept a local hotel. The victory over Bowker, not only showed the astounding control Driscoll possessed over a fight, a feature that was observed in almost all his subsequent engagements, but it cleaned up practically all the serious opposition at his weight and forced him to fight in the 9 stone class. First of all, however, he disposed of Jack Roberts for the second time, knocking him out in twelve rounds at Aberdare, then once more he returned to the National Sporting Club to meet Charlie Griffin, the officially recognised featherweight champion of Australia.

Griffin was a tough customer, but his boxing skill was not of the highest order. As early as the second round Driscoll had him on the end of a straight left and kept him there while the points were being rattled up. The Australian made strong efforts to get in close where his hard punching would have effect, but Jim stabbed him off and whenever he made him miss seized the opportunity to clip him neatly with the right. Griffin dropped further behind as the fight progressed without achieving any real success. In the fifteenth round, after having been warned by the referee, he used his head as a battering ram for want of a more effective weapon and was promptly disqualified.

The defeat of the Australian champion brought an offer from America and realising that there was more money to be made on the other side of the Atlantic, Driscoll set sail. In the States, he placed himself under the management of Charlie

Harvey, who was the guide, philosopher and friend of all visiting Britishers in those days. To say that he took America by storm would be putting it mildly. Jim's boxing skill was a revelation to New Yorkers and although most of his contests were supposed to be "no decision" affairs, he was credited by the newspaper critics as having had the better of each one. The men he met were the best featherweights in the world, their names being Matty Baldwin (twice), Grover Hayes (three times), Johnny Marto, Tommy Langdon, Leach Cross, and finally, the recognised world's champion, Abe Attell. In addition, while in the States. He boxed a return contest with Charlie Griffin, this time knocking him out in eleven rounds.

The fight with Attell took place on February 19, 1909, at New York, in the National Athletic Club. It was of ten rounds' duration with the no-decision rule applying. Between two such admitted masters of the craft nothing but a fine contest could result, and onlookers declared that it was impossible to conceive a fight containing more lessons in ringcraft. At this period of boxing an effort was being made to bring the sport back to a fairly respectable position, and this bout was one which did a lot towards this end. Men from all branches of life were among the spectators and there seemed to be something in the air which indicated that this was going to be a fight of fights.

The Welshman did not hesitate to show what he intended to do at the tap of the first bell. Driscoll was one of those rarities who pick out a particular spot for a target and then shoot both fists at that spot. He had a wonderful left hand, such as all high-class English fighters had in those days, and he began using that left hand on Attell's right eye. Now Abe Attell was never any slouch in the ring, and to land a left on his face was a matter that was sure to bring applause from the onlookers. There were a lot present at the ringside that night who never before had seen such a piston-like left hand as Driscoll possessed. He shot left after left into Attell's eye, and it was soon apparent that his plan of battle was to blind Attell

on the right side, and when a fighter is blind in one eye, he is a pretty easy mark for a clever boxer like Jim Driscoll. Attell could not block those lightning left punches that smote him with such regularity and his right eye was almost closed at the end of the second round.

But Driscoll did not rely entirely on his left jab to defeat Attell. He used his right with good effect, countering frequently on the face and sometimes in the stomach. Attell tried fighting for Driscoll's head, but most of his blows were either blocked or ducked. Rarely is there such an exhibition of blocking as Driscoll put up that night - he was about one of the cleverest duckers the ring has ever known. At one point Attell had the Welshman up against the ropes and it looked as if the American would eke out a lot of punishment before he could get away. But Jim ducked out as gracefully as a dancer just as Attell started a terrific right to the jaw. The punch was so viciously delivered that Attell was thrown to his knees. He expected that punch would land somewhere on Driscoll but it did not even fan him.

When the boys came into the seventh round Attell was in real fighting mood. He knew he had so far been outpointed and could not hope to outbox his clever rival. Instead he went in to make a slugging match of it. Driscoll led a left and Abe put over a right cross that just missed. Then Jim followed up with a succession of left hand jabs, but Attell bored in and landed a stiff left hook to the chin. This stung the Welshman into speedy retaliation and the two stood toe to toe for a while and exchanged punches freely in the middle of the ring.

Finally, the American caught his rival's right glove under his arm and held it, throwing repeated rights into Driscoll's mid-section until the referee ordered him to break. They came together again and once more Abe trapped Jim's right glove under his arm while he assailed the body. Driscoll protested to the referee who cautioned the American. This was Attell's only round and he tried hard to do as well in the next. But Driscoll's defence was too good and he had learned that it did not pay to mix it with his rival. Not only did he evade Attell's punches, but he retaliated with very telling blows to the head and body.

Realising that he had met his master, the champion fought like a demon and many times Driscoll only avoided danger by a clever piece of ducking or side-stepping. As it was he had to take many a nasty blow, but for every one he received two or more were given. Towards the end the American boxed at his best form and it took all the Welshman's superb ringcraft to keep out of trouble. He made sure of things by easily outspeeding and out-boxing the title-holder in the last round, at the end of which all but one of the newspaper men present gave the verdict to Driscoll, it being generally agreed that he had won the majority of the ten rounds. The next day one of the New York papers said, " Jim Driscoll leaves for home on the St. Paul today featherweight champion of the world. He outfought Abe Attell in seven out of ten rounds, whilst one of the others was even. Another critic said, "Abe Attell is no longer the premier featherweight boxer of the world. Jim Driscoll, of Cardiff, gained the honour last night. The little Briton opened the eyes of the crowd and closed one of Abe's." And here is a third opinion, "The winner left the ring without a mark, whereas Attell's right eye was bunged up and his nose spread over the face that for years had worn a championship smile."

Driscoll began packing his bag that night and no persuasion on the part of his American manager would induce him to stay. As a result of his victory offers came from all parts and he could have picked up a fortune within the next twelve months. But Jim was going back home to keep his word. "I promised to box for Nazareth House and they are expecting me," was all he would say. It was a charity show on behalf of children and each year he gave an exhibition at the tournament arranged for them. The lure of money meant nothing compared with keeping a promise and he sailed next day on the St. Paul, even leaving without his share of the Attell purse, which Harvey brought over some time afterwards.

It was nearly a year later when Driscoll next appeared in the ring in serious contest. Then the National Sporting Club matched him with Seaman Arthur Hayes for the vacant featherweight championship and the first of the Lord Lonsdale Challenge Belts awarded to that division. The contest took place on February 14, 1910, and lasted only six rounds by which time the sailor was in such a bad way that the referee stopped the contest. The following day Jim called at the Club by arrangement to be presented with his Belt, the little ceremony being attended by many well-known sportsmen and boxers. During one of the speeches mention was made that there would have to be some hard thinking in order to find another challenger for the Belt, when a voice said, "If Driscoll doesn't mind, I should like to box him. I happen to still be the undefeated featherweight champion of this country."

The speaker was Spike Robson, who had won the title

when defeating Johnny Summers in 1906, had never defended his laurels and was generally considered to have retired from the game. Since winning the British title he had been boxing principally in America where he had met the best featherweights in the world with a fair measure of success. He was a tough and fearless fighter, three years older than Driscoll and more experienced. Indeed, it was an ideal match and no time was lost in the signing of articles. In addition to the Lonsdale Belt and the 9 stone title, the stakes and purse money totalled £1,000, which was considered to be a stupendous sum in those days. The selected date was April 18, 1910.

For the first three rounds Driscoll used a straight left to such good effect that Robson hardly landed a blow of any note. Then in the fourth round, Spike swung a right from nowhere and Jim was too late in endeavouring to avoid it. The punch caught the Welshman flush on the left eye and promptly closed it. With one blow the whole prospects of the fight had changed and when Driscoll reached his corner it looked as if he would be compelled to give in. But, in spite of the fact that his seconds could do little to improve matters, Jim was determined to go on. As soon as the bell sounded to start the fifth session, Robson bounded out of his corner and rushed across the ring to put over a finishing blow. Seeing him coming, Driscoll slipped sideways off his stool and unable to check his headlong rush the challenger came into violent contact with the ring post, splitting open the scalp from which blood began to freely flow.

Although badly dazed from this accidental blow Robson pulled himself together and fought on grimly, but the happening had given Driscoll the respite he needed and within a round or two he began outpointing his rival in no uncertain manner. Spike continued to attack, but the Welshman began to take great toll of his rival with beautifully placed straight lefts to the face and right crosses to the chin. His boxing was superb - a classic exhibit - and by the fifteenth round Robson

was finished. By this time his resistance had gone and, opening out, Driscoll sent him to the canvas under a hail of well-directed blows from either hand. Spike took a count of "seven" but was soon down again and this time the referee called, "That will do, Driscoll." Jim had gained his second notch on the Belt.

Next, Driscoll made a return visit to the States, but only remained for one contest, a no-decision affair with Pal Moore. He had intended to fight a series of contests, but now a married man, he became homesick and returned to Cardiff. It was a great pity that he took this course, as apart from the fact that he was assured of earning some real money at last, it might have prevented him from partaking in a match that should never have been made and which resulted in the only blemish shown in his record. On his return frantic efforts were made to match him with his fellow-countryman, Fred Welsh, who was the British lightweight champion. The main idea behind this proposal was the fact that whereas Driscoll was an exponent of straight-left hitting and the upstanding British style, Welsh, who had picked up all his boxing knowledge in the States, adopted the crouch and was a round-arm hitter, and favoured close-quarter tactics.

Much harm was done by the supporters of both sides, who did what they could to stir up discord between the two rivals and succeeded very well. The match was made at 9 st. 6 lbs., a weight that brought Welsh to his true fighting poundage, whereas it meant that Driscoll had to give away the best part of half-a-stone - no mean handicap against a man of Freddy's ability. They fought for £2,500, of which £1,500 was to go to the winner. Actually, it was Driscoll who

received the larger sum, no doubt as some compensation for the weight he was being asked to give away. The contest aroused tremendous enthusiasm, in fact, from the time of making the contract until the two men entered the ring, there was little else talked about in Wales. They met at the American Rink, Cardiff, on December 20, 1910, and Mr. Bettinson, manager of the National Sporting Club, was appointed referee.

But the contest was a great disappointment. Welsh was out to spoil and did everything he could to prevent Driscoll from getting into his stride. Try as he might, Jim could not avoid going into the clinches which his rival sought at every opportunity, and at close-quarters Welsh brought off a variety of tricks that possessed nuisance value only. For the first time in his career, Driscoll lost his temper and after having been butted several times, he deliberately put his head under his opponent's chin and retaliated with no uncertainty. The referee had no other option than to disqualify Jim for a flagrant breach of the rules and Welsh was awarded victory in the tenth round.

The occurrence upset Driscoll for some time, but six weeks later he was performing in the National Sporting Club ring again, defending his title once more against Spike Robson. The latter had always maintained that he had been unlucky to lose at their first meeting and clamoured for a return fight. To this the Welshman readily agreed and they crossed gloves for the second time on January 30, 1911. Once again the challenger tried to carry the fight to his opponent and rushed in ferociously, only to be met by that unerring left that checked his progress with disconcerting regularity. Driscoll let him wear himself out, meanwhile putting up a wonderful display of perfect boxing. By the seventh session Robson was all in and after he had been floored several times the contest was stopped in Driscoll's favour. Jim had won the Lonsdale Belt outright in the record time of eleven-and-a-half months.

That was Driscoll's only fight in 1911 and in the two following years he took part in only two further engagements. In the first of these he met Jean Poesy, champion of France, their contest being for the European featherweight title. It took place at National Sporting Club, and was the annual Derby Week match, being staged on June 3, 1912. To coin a racing expression, it was a one-horse race. The Frenchman was strong and willing enough, but Driscoll boxed like a perfect machine and for the first half-dozen rounds did no more than send out his left into which Poesy ran as if attracted by a magnet. During the twelfth round, Jim feinted and his opponent made a wild lunge with his right, putting all his weight behind the blow. Like a flash Jim side-stepped, then as the French lad floundered forward he sent his famous right to the chin and dropped Poesy as if he had been shot. It was a perfect knockout.

"Peerless Jim's" only contest in 1913 was one of the hardest of his career. On January 27th he defended his British and World's titles against Owen Moran, one of the greatest featherweights who ever failed to win a championship. They met for an National Sporting Club purse and a special Belt, and everyone agreed that the man from Birmingham would give the Welshman the fight of his life. When Driscoll entered the ring he was not at his best in health and looked decided-

ly older than his thirty-three years. Moran was four years his junior and had trained to a hair. He was a bustling, two-handed scrapper, possessing plenty of boxing skill. Altogether a handful for anyone at the best of times and he caused Jim many anxious moments, especially towards the end of the twenty rounds' contest when Driscoll was fast tiring. In fact, the last round was the most thrilling of the lot and only the champion's amazing ringcraft saved him from being knocked out. The referee's decision was a "draw".

A return contest was demanded by Moran and his supporters, but before anything could be arranged Driscoll announced his retirement from the ring and the featherweight title was declared vacant. Jim spent his time in instructing others and brought many Welsh boxers to the fore, some of his protégés winning British titles for themselves. Then came the Great War and Jim immediately joined the Welsh Horse as a physical training instructor. Apart from teaching the men to box he gave exhibition after exhibition and there is no doubt that he worked far too hard. On many occasions he boxed with twenty or thirty men at each session and often was sent miles after that to give an exhibition or a demonstration. And it is not necessary to record that many army championships fell to the teams which came under Jim's supervision.

In 1919 the boxing world had a shock as well as a welcome surprise when Driscoll allowed himself to be persuaded into meeting the veteran Pedlar Palmer at Hoxton Baths, London. The affair was more an exhibition than a serious bout - at least it was supposed to be - but Palmer meant business and after four rounds the contest had to he stopped to save the "Box o' Tricks" from suffering any further punishment. It was an easy victory for Driscoll for he had not extended himself in the slightest. During his army career he had developed stomach trouble which caused him to be very careful of everything he ate and he found this painful malady to be steadily sapping his stamina and strength.

The result of the match with Palmer, however, encouraged him to try again to make a comeback and three weeks later he boxed twenty rounds at Mountain Ash with a fellow Welshman, Francis Rossi. The latter was a very promising youngster who put up a good show but only stayed the full distance because Driscoll was so painfully off-colour. He was but a shadow of his former great self but even so the verdict of a "draw" favoured Rossi more than it did his opponent. Most people imagined that " Peerless Jim" would give up after this poor display, but he had given his word to the National Sporting Club that he would fight his last contest there - and Driscoll always kept his word. His selected opponent was the youthful Charles Ledoux, bantamweight champion of France, and the weight was fixed at 8 st. 12 lbs., a poundage that suited the Welshman, who had lost weight because of his stomach trouble.

But if the weight suited Driscoll the distance was definitely to his detriment. The French party insisted on the contest being for twenty rounds because they realised that over a short distance it would be a walk-over for the Britisher. Jim's friends pleaded with him to insist on a shorter contest but he would not argue; it was to be his last fight and he had only to keep on his feet to win. And for nearly fifteen rounds he kept to his resolution. Ledoux was out-boxed in every department except gameness and apart from an occasional swing to the body scarcely laid a glove on his veteran opponent.

The contrast between the two men was most marked. Jim stood up straight in truly classic pose, while Ledoux was bent over, his nose almost touching his knee. Feinting almost contemptuously Driscoll drew the Frenchman's attack, slipped it and sent a left into the face. Ledoux plunged in, but found his body shots blocked and could do nothing. He went back, circled round and sought openings. Then, fancying he had discovered one, would dash in, but was blocked and pushed off by Jim's shoulder as he tried to bore his way in close. The crowded National Sporting Club roared its amazed approval and amused relish at the ease with which "Peerless Jim" made his opponent miss, twisted him round, made him look foolish, and hit his younger and stronger rival almost when, where, and how he chose.

Time and again at the close of each round, Driscoll would stroll back to his corner the undisputed monarch of pugilism, while Ledoux had to gaze after him in speechless admiration. Not only was the distance just five rounds too long, but in addition, Jim was suffering internal agonies, and to add to his misfortunes his left thumb which had been knocked up accidentally in training was again damaged, putting his left hand

almost out of action. He tried his hardest to hide the fact, but the Frenchman soon became aware that he was only being tapped with the left and by biding his time and hitting out desperately at every opportunity, began to wear his rival down with body blows.

Driscoll, who had perhaps discovered that his legs were giving way, went in to hit Ledoux harder in the fifteenth round. He was still scoring merrily and conscious that he had won every round up to date, when one of his rival's fierce right swings landed on the side of Jim's head. The blow shook the thirty-nine-year-old veteran badly and he lacked the vitality to recover. The Frenchman saw that his chance had arrived and punched away from all angles. The Welshman was too shaken to retaliate, but he could still twist and turn his head and duck and swerve. Ledoux kept up a non-stop battery of blows and strove with all his might to drop the older man, but Jim kept out of serious danger until the bell, and had just strength enough to stagger to his stool. He had escaped a knockout but the end had come.

The sixteenth round was signalled and the gallant Driscoll responded to the call. He could only stagger out to meet his rival and his seconds, seeing that he was now practically helpless, threw in their towels. Jim wanted to carry on, but Ledoux refused. He could not bear to hit such a marvel and the drama was closed by Driscoll's seconds carrying the old hero from the scene of his glories and greatest triumphs. In his dressing-room after the fight, Ledoux remarked, "Driscoll is the master. The greatest man I have ever met or ever shall meet. He played with me for fourteen-and-a-half rounds and I could do nothing."

"Peerless Jim" definitely retired after this. A national testimonial was formed and subscriptions to same amounted to over £5,000, so beloved and appreciated was Driscoll among the sporting fraternity. This sum, together with his earnings as a referee and the money he received for writing a weekly boxing article would have kept Jim in comfort, but he was not allowed to enjoy his retirement. The stomach trouble developed into ulcers and the condition became worse as time went on. On January 30, 1925, Driscoll died in hospital. He had just passed his forty-fourth birthday. From an early hour on the morning of his funeral, van-loads of wreaths arrived at his home. They filled up the place until the never-ending stream of tributes had to be temporarily diverted to neighbours' houses. It was a military  funeral, but at the request of many old friends the gun-carriage was dispensed with until the cortege was in close proximity to the cemetery, two miles from the house, the coffin being carried on willing shoulders.

I have styled Jim Driscoll, the "King of Cardiff". His monarchy was proclaimed to all on this day. Cardiff stopped work entirely, traffic in the main streets was held up because of the thousands who followed the coffin, while scores of thousands of mourners lined the streets. The cemetery gates had to be closed to stem the rush of sympathisers, all anxious to see the last of "Our Jim". The "king" had died. He may have had equally honoured and mourned predecessors, though this is to be doubted. He has had no successor, even approaching his majesty and there would appear to be scant likelihood of any.

www.ingramcontent.com/pod-product-compliance
Lightning Source LLC
Chambersburg PA
CBHW050843160426
43192CB00011B/2129